365 WAYS
TO GIVE THANKS

365 WAYS
TO GIVE THANKS

One for Every Day of the Year

BRENDA SHOSHANNA, PH.D.

A Birch Lane Press Book
Published by Carol Publishing Group

Carol Publishing Group edition, 1999

A Birch Lane Press Book
Published by Carol Publishing Group
Birch Lane Press is a registered trademark of Carol Communications, Inc.

Editorial, sales and distribution, and rights and permissions inquiries should be
addressed to Carol Publishing Group, 120 Enterprise Avenue, Secaucus, N.J. 07094
In Canada: Canadian Manda Group, One Atlantic Avenue, Suite 105, Toronto,
Ontario M6K 3E7

Carol Publishing Group books may be purchased in bulk at special discounts for
sales promotion, fund-raising, or educational purposes. Special editions can be
created to specifications. For details, contact Special Sales Department, Carol
Publishing Group, 120 Enterprise Avenue, Secaucus, N.J. 07094.

Manufactured in the United States of America
10 9 8 7 6 5 4 3 2

Library of Congress Cataloging-in-Publication Data

Shoshanna, Brenda.
    365 ways to give thanks : one for every day of the year / by Brenda Shoshanna.
        p.   cm.
    "A Birch Lane Press book."
    ISBN 1–55972–475–7 (hardcover)
    1. Gratitude.   I. Title.
BF575.G68S46   1998
394.2—DC21   98–20499
                                                            CIP

This book is dedicated to Zöe and Remy,
and all the wonderful children who sparkle
naturally, and give thanks just by being who they are.

CONTENTS

ACKNOWLEDGMENTS

I wish to offer special thanks and acknowledgment to my incredible agent Noah Lukeman, without whom this book would never have been written. I give thanks for his strength, perseverance, inspiration, and endless creativity. I also thank my excellent editor Hillel Black for his fine efforts and assistance.

I also wish to particularly thank Daniel Myerson, who contributed many ways of giving thanks, and whose nature is to be a source of constant joy.

I thank, too, Joshua, Adam, Melissa, Abram, and Gerry, for their ongoing love and support.

INTRODUCTION

*Inasmuch as ye have done it unto one of the least of these my brethren,
ye have done it unto me.*

—MATTHEW 26:40

There are hundreds of large and small ways to give thanks. Usually we are so preoccupied with dwelling on what we are deprived of, it never occurs to us to give thanks for what we've received. We do not notice the gifts and blessings that surround us; rather, we take most of them as our due.

When we start to give thanks continually, these gifts expand. The more we give them to others, the more we receive. The more we give thanks, the more joyous our life becomes.

The different ways of giving thanks suggested in this book can be done on the day specified, or any other day. Some of the holidays mentioned are celebrated on different dates each year. Most of them, however, are celebrated during the month in which they are mentioned.

In the world to come all prayers will cease.
But the prayer of Thanksgiving will not.

—Talmud

To see what is right and not do it is
want of courage.

—Confucious

365 WAYS
TO GIVE THANKS

JANUARY 1

New Year's Day

Find someone you have not yet forgiven. Call that person up and forgive them. Start over again for the new year.

No year should start with traces of resentment hanging in the air. The greatest gift you can give yourself and others is the gift of forgiveness, which washes both the giver and the receiver clean. Forgiveness clears the way for future good to come to you. It reminds the person you have forgiven that people can transcend pettiness and start the new year with joy.

Think of a family member, friend, acquaintance, or someone at work with whom you have had a disagreement. It need not be something serious, perhaps a mistake or a current irritation. Call the person up and talk it over. Don't cast blame. Listen to his or her side of the story patiently and explain that you want to wipe the slate clean for the new year. See how wonderful you both feel.

JANUARY 2

Go through your calendar and fill in the dates of all your friends', family's and acquaintances' birthdays so that you can remember them all year long.

Spend time today writing down the birthdays of those with whom you are close. Then make another list of more casual friends and acquaintances. Everyone loves to have their birthday remembered.

The very next birthday on your list, pick up the phone and sing happy birthday to that person. You'll both have a good laugh and he or she will feel touched.

Keep your birthday list where you can see it. Check it and add to it regularly. Be sure to make that singing call when the important days come.

JANUARY 3

At the end of each day write down on a calendar the best thing that happened to you that day.

So many of our victories and small delights drift out of our minds or pass by unnoticed. Taking the time each day to write them down and keep them where you can see them makes a big difference.

Purchase a lovely calendar you can hang up, and at the end of each day, write down the best thing that happened to you that day. Write it in large letters.

As you do this day by day, you will soon have quite a collection of happy memories. Looking back over them will serve to inspire and remind you of how fortunate you have been.

At the end of the year, you can keep the calendar handy, and as the next year rolls along (and you're working on your new calendar), you can check back over the past year and see what happened to you that very day. You will find doing so fascinating and uplifting.

JANUARY 4

Bring a toy to a child in the hospital.

We live walled-off lives, hiding behind the illusion that we cannot do much to help the enormous suffering in the world. But every act makes a difference. Start with one act today. There is a child at a local hospital who would be greatly uplifted by receiving a gift.

Call your local hospital and contact Volunteer Services. They will tell you the steps to take to bring a gift to a sick child. The gift might be a book, puzzle, crayons, clay, a coloring book, or a puppet. More importantly, spend some time at the youngster's bedside. What the gift is, is not as important as the fact that someone unknown is thinking of the child. Your act of kindness will help this child believe in the unexpected goodness of life. For all you know, you could even contribute to the youngster's healing.

Throw a dinner party for those who have been giving to you. This can include friends, colleagues, and loved ones. Publicly thank them at the party.

Many give and have no idea of the effect that their behavior has on others. Stopping to publicly thank them, as well as going to the trouble to prepare a dinner and invite others, will not allow them to brush off the contribution they have been making.

The dinner could be a barbecue, sandwiches and salad, formal, or even just coffee, dessert, or drinks. You do not have to announce your intention ahead of time. Once all are gathered, you can then thank them for the good they have done. An evening like this is an affirmation for all of you. You will see that in the act of giving, *you* receive the most.

Speak kindly to someone who's angry with you.

It's so easy to respond with anger and harsh words when someone expresses anger toward you, especially if you feel it is not warranted. But anger begets anger. Harsh words close doors between people. Try something different today. Listen to the angry person and find kind words to say in response. You might say, "I understand, I'm sorry you feel that way," or "It's upsetting to be so angry."

Wait until the anger has passed and then calmly discuss the situation. Although the kind words may not solve the problem immediately, they will create the possibility for future discussion and prevent things from getting worse.

While out walking on the street today spend at least five minutes picking up litter you see lying around.

We are so accustomed to litter that no one thinks it is their responsibility to take the time to clean it up. But every street or road that you clean yourself will become meaningful to you.

You can do this casually, on the way to work, or you can make it more elaborate, taking a large trash bag along. Bending over and picking up litter as you walk is also wonderful exercise. After you've walked for just a few minutes, the bag will probably be half full. And maybe, while you're not looking, someone else might see what you're doing and devote a few minutes to helping.

Can you imagine if ten people picked up litter? Fifteen? A hundred?

In a meaningful way, make a point of thanking anyone who does anything to serve you today.

We seldom notice the many, many ways we are constantly being served all day long. Instead, we dwell on the little annoyances and disappointments. When you start paying attention to the services you receive, when you stop and really see the person who is performing that service, and you take the time to say thanks, your entire day will change.

Some of the people you might want to start thanking include someone who holds a door for you, a waitress who serves you lunch, or a person on the phone who has been especially helpful. You might want to include people who are seldom thanked, such as telephone operators, post office workers, train conductors, newspaper vendors, or perhaps even a child who has made you smile.

People will start to look beautiful. Strangers will turn into friends.

Take someone to a ball game.

If you think about it, there must be at least ten friends, business colleagues, or acquaintances who would love to go to a ball game. How come you haven't asked them? Is it just because it's not part of your routine?

Break old routines. Try something different. Make a list of the people you think would like to go. Call up Ticketmaster or check your local newspaper today. Find out the schedule. Pick a few alternate dates.

Call the people on your list and see who is available. Then extend an invitation to the game. The person will be completely delighted. So will you.

You'll both enjoy being playful together. You'll probably enjoy it so much, it will become part of a new routine.

When getting a sandwich for lunch, buy an extra one and give it to a beggar.

Almost everywhere we go, there are homeless people. Most of the time they seem bothersome. We often brush them aside. It's not so difficult to buy an extra sandwich, at least once, and give it to a hungry person.

When you go out for lunch or breakfast, just ask for two bagels or sandwiches instead of one. Get two cups or coffee, or two glasses of juice. By giving food instead of money, you can at least be sure that your gift will not be used for drugs or alcohol.

Never be afraid that you're giving to someone who's faking it or doesn't deserve it. Remember this quote from the Bible: "Never fear giving to a false beggar. You, yourself, are a false beggar before God."

The measure by which you give, is the measure by which you receive.

—TORAH

JANUARY 11

Put a candy bar or a piece of candy in the mailbox for your mailman.

Who thinks of the mailman as he makes his daily rounds, taking care of us? What mailman expects to be rewarded with a delicious candy, a moment of thankfulness? What a nice surprise for him to find it and know that someone is thinking of him, and is grateful for the service he's performing. How wonderful for you, too, if you should be lucky enough to catch his smile.

JANUARY 12

Take a child to the park today.

Often we stay at home with our children and spend too much time watching TV or playing computer games. Break the pattern and take your child to the park.

Spend at least an hour there. Push your child on a swing, play in the sandbox, bring a box lunch, feed the birds, play catch. Buy an ice cream.

Children thrive on personal attention. Even a little of it means a great deal. If a child receives attention on an ongoing basis, a new world will open for that child. A new world will also open for you. There is no end to the wealth of pleasure a child can bring.

Make something with your hands you've never made before. Give it to someone you care for, for no reason at all.

We think we need reasons to give presents, or that a gift must be expensive and well wrapped. The best presents are always those that are made personally for someone you are thinking about. These gifts live long afterward, expressing our inner heart of thanks.

A present could be as simple as a drawing, collage, paper flowers, something whittled in wood, seashells found at the beach strung together, or something you've painted on a rock.

They could be as elaborate as a knit sweater, model airplane, wooden table, beautiful carving, hanging tapestry, wooden box, or a woven blanket for a bed.

By making something with your hands that you've never made before, you can reach into the well of your inner creativity and discover something new about yourself. When you make a present for someone, you are giving it to yourself as well.

Think of someone in the office who has been supportive of you. Let them know.

We often refrain from acknowledging how supportive someone else has been, especially in an office situation, for fear it will be taken the wrong way or seem unnecessary. We usually take it for granted that the person knows how we feel anyway.

Stop for a moment and turn this around. The person could be a secretary, office peer, or even the boss. No matter what his or her role in our lives is, everyone thrives on grateful words.

Most people have no idea how you're feeling. Most don't even realize their support has been noticed. Making a point of acknowledging that another person has made a difference in your life not only will uplift that individual, but also reinforce the goodness available to you.

Martin Luther King Jr.'s Birthday

Practice nonviolence in honor of Martin Luther King Jr. Tell others about it.

On this day we honor the memory of Martin Luther King Jr., a black leader who rallied a nation with his great vision, presence, and call to peace. He is famous for many of his speeches and actions, particularly his statement, "I have a dream." In honor of his memory, let us carry on his dream of nonviolence and peace.

King said, "Nonviolence is the answer to the crucial political and moral questions of our time; the need for man to overcome oppression and violence without resorting to oppression and violence. Man must evolve for all human conflict a method which rejects revenge, aggression and retaliation. The foundation for such a method is love."

Discover ways to carry out Martin Luther King Jr.'s dream in your personal life. Reject revenge and aggression. Find ways to resolve conflict with others carefully and peacefully so everyone can feel loved.

Send a friend an e-mail today saying you're thinking of him or her.

It's easy enough to send e-mail. There are plenty of friends out there we take for granted day in and day out. We think they'll always be there for us, whether we reach out to them or not. We don't think it's our job to make them feel special.

Try changing this today. Take a few minutes at your computer and drop your friend an e-mail. Say you're thinking of him or her. Leave a world of smiles all around.

Help someone who's having difficulty with their bags at the airport.

For many people, travel is stressful, especially if they go alone. They are no longer in familiar surroundings and can feel unprotected, uncomfortable, or at a loss.

Offer to lend a hand. Perhaps you can wait with them for a taxi, or help carry their bags while they get to their car.

The person will feel so much better entering a possibly unknown place, if there is at least one friend or stranger who will help.

Offer some classes or instruction in your special skills to needy children or adults.

We all have special skills or knowledge that we can impart to others to help them along. Figure out what you have to teach that would be useful to adults or children, and then offer some classes, workshops, or instruction free of charge to those in need. Learning the skills that you'll teach might help the individual get a new or better job. The skills you could teach might include typing, musical instruments, computers, singing, mechanics, building, cooking, writing, public speaking, or hand crafts.

To find out who might profit by this, and how you can reach them, call your local church, temple, or school district. You can also contact the Salvation Army or shelters for the homeless.

Set up a recycling system in your home for paper, plastic, and glass.

The environment is a mother to us. We must take care of her. If we are careless about refuse, our soil, oceans, and forests will be depleted, depriving us of nourishment.

Making a difference starts with one person. Over a lifetime of recycling, you can single-handedly save massive quantities of material, while helping to stop pollution. More importantly, you'll be part of the solution, not the problem.

Call up your local office of the Environmental Protection Agency and tell them you want to recycle. They will give you the information, schedule, and supplies you need. Once you get into the habit, it becomes routine.

By consciously taking care of our garbage, we can help Mother Earth stay healthy and strong.

Build a huge snowman for all who pass by to enjoy. (If there's no snow, make some other decoration to cheer up the neighborhood.)

We live in an impersonal world. The streets we walk on do not speak to us. You can change this dreary condition for those who pass by your home by making a charming snowman. If you can't do this, find another way to decorate your space. You can put up balloons, wreaths of dried flowers on your door, or plant a beautiful front garden. You can build a rock garden, make a sculpture, or hang stained-glass figures in the window. Why not place a lovely welcome mat out where others can see it, or decorate your mailbox? Include your family's ideas as well. It will be as if you are reaching out to strangers who pass, putting a smile on their face and telling them to have a wonderful day.

Find out more about Oriental culture in honor of the Chinese and Korean New Year.

The Oriental New Year, which falls between January 21 and February 19 every year, is celebrated with great festivals, including several days of parades, fireworks, and feasts. The fireworks serve to ward off evil spirits and bring in a year of health and prosperity.

If these festivities are taking place in your area, see if you can attend the parade. Spend time speaking to some Oriental individuals in your area about their customs and how they, specifically, are going to be celebrating this year.

As we reach out to those of different cultures and get to know them as individuals, we are helping to eradicate prejudice and build a better world for all.

Before eating a meal, take a moment to be really grateful for the food.

Many feel that food is their birthright. They consume much of their food mechanically and rarely stop to savor it. Also, few consider the trouble many, many people took getting the food to them.

Consider the tuna sandwich in front of you: Before it came to your table, a farmer grew and harvested the wheat for bread; the fish had to be caught by fishermen; the tomatoes and lettuce were grown and picked. Think of all the packaging and distribution people involved in this enormous chain.

Stop, breathe deeply, and be grateful for it all.

Surprise your doorman with a little present.

Your doorman stands patiently in front of your building all day long, waiting to serve you. Few think of serving him, too. If you stop and buy him a magazine, soda, or cassette tape, think how delighted and touched he will be. Serving must go both ways to be truly fulfilling.

Give, give recklessly. We are only part of
an endless process with nothing to gain or lose.
—HENRY MILLER

Tell a child a story. Let them ask you all the questions they want. Find some good answers.

Children love and need to hear stories. Their minds are fertile ground for fantasy, curiosity, and new ways of seeing life.

Go to the library or children's section of a bookstore and pick out a few books in the right age range for the child to whom you are reading. Certain books are all-time classics. If you are not acquainted with the titles, your librarian or bookseller can assist you.

Bring the books home and read them out loud to the child or make up some stories of your own. If the child interrupts and asks questions, let him or her do so, and then ask for the child's own answers or provide your own. Some children want to hear the same story repeatedly. It doesn't mean they do not understand. It just means that this is their way of deeply drinking it all in.

The time spent telling a story to a child can amaze you, and make you search within yourself for truths you didn't realize you knew.

Go through your photos. Choose one that is special, get it framed, and send it to the people in it. (If you don't have a picture like this, take one.)

This is a simple but deeply moving gift. People love photographs and memories of special moments and friends. It's easy to take photographs and then file them away in some album.

When you buy a special frame for a photo and send it to the people in it, it will have a lasting value for them. If you don't have a picture like that, make a point of taking one next time someone special is visiting you. Then frame it and send it along.

Many of those who receive this photo will hang it up, see it daily, and thank you over and over in their hearts.

If it's cold out and someone is working on the street near your home, possibly a construction man, a gardener, or a landscaper, offer that person a warm drink.

Often we see others working outdoors in cold weather right near our home. It only takes a few moments to make some coffee, tea, or hot chocolate, bring it outdoors with some cups, and offer it to that person. How good this drink will feel.

The same is true in very hot weather. When you see others laboring outdoors in the heat, why not offer some iced tea, lemonade, or other cool drink?

Sit down and write a poem and give it as a gift to a friend, family member, or someone you love. (If you feel uncomfortable writing your own poem, find a poem you like, write it down, and send it.)

It seems very difficult to write a poem, but doing so is actually simple. A poem is just a way to see the world from your unique point of view. Today, sit down and write whatever comes to mind about the afternoon, the morning, or the way you feel at night. Write a few lines about your neighbor, dreams, or the way the wind feels on your face. (Go to the library and take out a book of poems if you wish to get some ideas.)

Decide to whom you are going to give your poem. Then write a few lines about that person, too. What makes them special? (If you find it impossible to write something down, pick out a poem in a book that says it for you).

Choose the best poem you've either written, or found, fold it beautifully, tie it with a ribbon, and give it to your friend.

If someone loans you their car, fill their gas tank when you're finished with it. (You can also look for an excuse to borrow someone's car so you can do this.)

Do you ever have the opportunity to borrow someone's car? Is there someone in your family, or a close friend, who lets you have the keys? How do you thank or repay them?

Today, take their car to the gas station and fill the tank to the limit. Don't say a word to them about it. Think how delighted they'll be the next time they get behind the wheel.

(To take this to the next step, if you borrow their car regularly, or if you feel so inclined, you might also take their car to be washed.)

So often we take for granted the things we have been loaned. We may return the thing we borrowed in the same condition we've received it, but how many times do we return it a little better than before?

Contact the Make a Wish Foundation and see how you can be of help.

The Make a Wish Foundation grants terminally ill children their final wishes. Children, or families of terminally ill children, write to the foundation with the child's special wish. The foundation then proceeds to do all they can to grant the wish, including making travel arrangements for the child.

There are many ways in which you can help support the foundation's efforts. Contact the office in your area and see what you can do.

Shovel the snow on your neighbor's walk.

Has it snowed recently? Does your neighbor need help with the snow on his walk? While shoveling your own snow, extend yourself a little: Reach out and shovel your neighbor's walk. (If your neighbor doesn't need the help, find someone else on the block who does and extend a helping hand.)

When you see a child today, make him laugh.

We often pass children by, in restaurants, through car windows, walking on the street, or shopping at the store. Stop for a moment today and acknowledge the youngster. Surprise the child by making a funny face so he or she can laugh. If the child doesn't laugh, find some other way to delight him or her. Rustle your keys, wave hello, blow a kiss. Let the child know the world can be a fun place.

Find out about the Peace Corps and if it is something you might like to join one day. Tell others about it.

The Peace Corps is a government-funded organization that sponsors individuals who wish to volunteer approximately two years (twenty-seven months) to work in a developing nation with those in need. Volunteers, who must be at least eighteen years old and a U.S. citizen, work in education, business, agriculture, the environment, and health education. They are given a stipend to cover living expenses.

The Peace Corps is presently in eighty-five countries where they have been invited to come and help. Some places include Russia, Lithuania, Central Asia, Africa, West Africa, and the Ivory Coast.

Participating in a program such as this is a profound way of giving thanks for the good you have received by living in a country with the resources and opportunities of the United States. It is also a wonderful way of expanding your knowledge and gaining experience with people and life in other lands.

For more information, call the Peace Corps directly.

FEBRUARY 1

Black History Month

Attend a film, concert, or play that deals with African-American culture. Listen to music performed by black artists or read a book by a black author.

This entire month celebrates black history and culture. There have been many outstanding African-American individuals who have contributed to our culture, including Muhammed Ali, Maya Angelou, Hattie McDaniel, Toni Morrison, Miles Davis, Lorraine Hansberry, and Colin Powell, among others.

Learn more about the black experience by attending a film or play that deals with it, such as *The Color Purple* by Alice Walker, or *Raisin in the Sun* by Lorraine Hansberry. Read the writings of significant black authors such as Toni Morrison or Eldrige Cleaver. Listen to the music of Miles Davis, Duke Ellington, or Thelonious Monk. Share these experiences with others. By understanding black history and experience more fully, we are recognizing and giving thanks to African Americans for their talents and contributions.

FEBRUARY 2

At a wedding, or other place where people are dancing, suggest to your husband or boyfriend that he ask the woman who has been sitting alone all night for a dance.

Most of the time we are unaware of how lonely one can feel as a single person at a wedding, party, dance, or family function where others are dancing. That person watches others who seem happy together and feels his or her loneliness even more keenly. One dance can help that person feel a part of the celebration.

Most people are usually very possessive of their partners. But if you are willing to share for a dance or two, your partner will only respect and love you more.

If somebody gives you too much change when you buy something, make sure you give the change back. Or, if somebody has overpaid you, don't let it slip by.

It is easy to overlook mispayment and pocket the money. We might justify doing so by saying we deserve it, or we were meant to get the extra cash. But in doing so, we do not realize that the individual who made the error usually has to pay it back out of his or her own pocket at the end of the day. This can easily become a hardship for someone.

Be careful with other people's money. If there is an error, be sure to make amends.

Fill a gift basket with treats and bring it to your neighbor.

In the middle of winter, when the days are cold and night falls early, why not surprise a neighbor with a gift for no reason? Fill up a basket with dates, nuts, dried fruit, and a small homemade banana bread. Tie it with a ribbon and bring it over. Your neighbor will experience the welcome warmth of your heart.

**You or your child should start to learn a
musical instrument, painting, writing,
dancing, or any of the arts.**

We all have the ability to be creative, though many of us have stifled it. When we are open to our own creative abilities, we receive many ways of realizing and expressing the joy of life and giving thanks for it.

Make a point of helping your child, or yourself, get started on learning a musical instrument, painting, drawing, writing, dancing, or any other creative expression that feels right. Not only will you add richness to your lives, but as you and your child develop your talents, you will have much richness to share with others.

Walk in someone else's shoes.

Is there someone in your life you're having a problem with, someone that you feel compelled to criticize and judge? Does their behavior irritate you and you're not exactly sure why?

Do something different today. When you think of that person, instead of becoming upset, imagine that you are them. Think of what it feels like to go through their day. Put yourself in their shoes.

This simple exercise is extremely powerful. Rather than sitting in judgment, we look at that person from the inside out. Compassion often develops. At the very least, harsh feelings melt away.

> *You cannot truly know a man*
> *Until you've walked a hundred miles*
> *In his moccasins.*
>
> —NATIVE AMERICAN SAYING

Buy an inspiring bumper sticker and put it on the back of your car.

To be stuck in traffic is annoying for everyone. We sit staring at the car in front of us and think about all the things we could be doing. If there is a bumper sticker on the back of your car with a cheerful statement, the person behind you will have to smile. You'll attract their attention and brighten their day.

Some sayings you can use are "Everyday's a Good Day"; "Remember the Moment You Felt the Best"; or "Choose Love—You Can't Make a Wrong Turn."

Learn a few jokes and tell them.

It's very easy to brighten up a dull conversation or distract someone who's been complaining too long. Learn a few jokes and find a way to slip them into the conversation.

There are many collections of jokes that you can find at a library or bookstore. Spend an hour copying the jokes that suit you. Then go home and memorize them. The next time you are stuck in a conversation that's going downhill, find a way to slip in one of your jokes. You'll be amazed at how quickly the mood changes.

After you've done this a few times, return to the book and learn a few more jokes.

If someone has a complaint against you, really listen to him or her.

Often we tune out when another person starts to complain. We pretend we're listening, but our eyes glaze over. Inside, our heart glazes over too. We nod our head and smile when we're supposed to, but we're really not there.

Change this behavior today. When someone has a complaint against you, really listen to that person. Try not to judge him or her. Don't judge yourself either. When blame begins, listening ends. Try to understand what need that person is expressing. See if you can find some way to meet it or to correct the situation that person is having difficulty with.

When you are able to listen in this manner, not only will your relationship deepen, but you will grow.

Appreciate three things about yourself.

Day after day we take ourselves for granted. Just like anyone else, we too need to be appreciated and acknowledged. We are like another person to ourselves. A kind word, a little gift, or a moment of appreciation from ourselves to ourselves works wonders during the day.

Write down three things today that you appreciate about yourself. Some examples could be that you keep your word to others, that you know how to take a joke, and that even when you may be stressed, you make that extra effort to think of someone else. Take time to read them aloud. Take them in. Breathe. Give yourself thanks for being exactly who you are.

FEBRUARY 11

Do not dwell on losses. Dwell on all the good that's here now.

Some of us become preoccupied with what we have lost, and we use these losses as a reason not to live fully now. We feel if we keep thinking of the past, somehow it will come back. In this manner, we lose our precious *nows*.

Make a point of not dwelling on what you have lost, but on all the good that is presently here. If you find yourself dwelling on the past too much, turn your attention to the present. Each day make a list of those who are here with you now, and how you might be of help to them.

When we focus on giving to others, our personal sense of loss subsides, and the present becomes vital again.

FEBRUARY 12
Lincoln's Birthday

List five things you receive from this country and five things you can do in return. Do one of them today.

This is a time to celebrate one of the great men of our nation. Stop for a moment and think of what it means to you to be a citizen of the United States. What would your life be like somewhere else, without the freedoms we take for granted?

If we focus on a few simple actions, we can have some kind of impact, small though it may be. If everyone does this, the impact grows quickly.

List at least five things you can do to give back to your country. Some ideas might involve volunteering in a political campaign. Contact your local political party and ask if there is some help they need. Write a letter to an editor about your views, or contact your congressman about a particular issue. You might help get people out to the polls when it's time to vote.

Pick one item on your list and do it today. You might feel so good and connected, you'll want to do a few more.

Introduce two people you know who are lonely.

Many people are afraid to introduce others for fear a possible relationship won't work out. They do not realize how grateful others will be for the opportunity to meet a new friend. Most of all, they will be touched that you care about their happiness.

If you don't know who is or isn't lonely, ask some friends if they know someone who is alone and would rather not be. With just a little effort, you'll soon discover quite a few people in this situation. You'll be amazed to discover that most lonely people are grateful just for companionship.

Choose two individuals who seem well suited, and arrange for them to meet in a way that suits them both. Some would just like a phone number, and will do the rest themselves; others would feel better meeting at a small gathering. In that case, invite a few people for coffee and include them as well.

Whether they hit it off is up to them. The fact that you will have extended a helping hand is what matters most.

Draw or paint a special card for someone you love. Name three things that have been given to you that have meant a lot.

Just the fact that you've stopped to spend time making your own Valentine greeting, personalizing it with specific memories and statements of the gifts you received from a loved one, is an act of love.

You can make the card unusual too. For example, take the back of a Valentine candy box that is shaped like a heart, cut out and paste pictures you like in it, and write your special thoughts in the middle. Wrap it up in a lace bow and send it to someone you love.

This will remind you of why you hold that person dear.

Love beautifies the giver and elevates the receiver.

—SWAMI SHIVANANDA

Express your gratitude to your local firemen.

Most of us have no idea of the bravery, sacrifice, and sense of duty that firemen live with every day. They constantly give of themselves to the community especially in times of danger or during emergencies.

How many times do we stop to thank them? Let's do it today. There are many ways this can be accomplished. You can send some money, a box of candy, a plant, some books, magazines, cassette players, tickets to the movies, or a long letter of recognition and thanks. Whatever you choose to do for firemen, just the fact that they are remembered will mean a lot.

Give an extra big tip to a waiter, waitress, or cab driver.

Unexpected generosity goes a long way. How aware are we of the people who serve us in difficult jobs? How much would it take to give them an unexpectedly large tip one day? They could certainly use the extra few dollars but, more than that, it will lift their spirits and help them feel hopeful about the essential goodness of humankind.

Give any extra clothes you have and are not using to the Police Athletic League or to the homeless.

Go through your closet and take out any old clothes that no longer fit you or that you have not worn for the past year or two. Gather them together and give them away.

Call your local Police Athletic League and local shelters for the homeless and ask where the clothing can be dropped off. Your old garments will then be given to those less fortunate who are in need.

Sponsor a child.

It is relatively inexpensive to sponsor a foreign child. In some cases, donating as little as $25.00 a month will pay toward a child's food, schooling and clothing in a foreign country. Needless to say, this donation can help give a whole new life to a youngster.

The child will correspond with you, and you will be kept informed of how the child is getting along. This generous act will have immense consequences. Different agencies, such as ORT, Save the Children, and World Crisis Network, help deal with these children. Find an agency you feel good about, contact them, and get all the details.

Give a friend a massage. Get one for yourself.

Our body is our temple. It serves us day after day in hundreds of ways. How much do you do for your body in return? Do you have a means of regularly releasing the tension and exhaustion that build up?

A massage is a wonderful gift to give to a friend and also to yourself. It can be a time of close sharing with a friend and profound restfulness for you. It enables us to give back to the muscles and tissues themselves by offering them time to unwind and repair.

If someone is being publicly abused, defend them.

Sometimes when we are out with friends, an individual in our group can become the butt of laughter and scorn. This is very painful to the individual.

At a moment like this, having a public ally in the group can be a great gift. It can also stop the process from going farther and causing more damage.

Speak up. Find out good things about the person being criticized, and announce them publicly. Let everyone know you won't tolerate seeing someone being hurt.

Throw a welcoming party for someone new on the block or in your apartment building.

Moving into a new neighborhood can be nerve wracking. It is a time of transition and change. There is nothing more wonderful than to feel welcomed, to feel you are not a stranger anymore. A block can be like a family, or it can remain a collection of strangers. It is up to you.

You can provide a simple welcome party by supplying coffee, cake, or dessert, and inviting people in the neighborhood to join you. Not only will the new people feel wonderful, but others who are invited will have a chance to renew their relationships as well. The thoughtfulness being expressed will be appreciated by all.

Become aware of the gift of independence this country has granted to you.

Think carefully about what independence means to you. Describe the freedom and independence you have as a result of living in this country.

Look at the ways in which you might inadvertently withhold freedom and independence from others. Some examples might be the freedom of speech and freedom to be different. Can you tolerate different points of view? Are you willing to listen when others express opinions different from yours?

Grant someone else a freedom today that you haven't given them before. Let that person express to you whatever is truly on his or her mind.

Help an old person cross the street.

We always assume others can get along on their own. But right under our eyes, if we open them and look, are elderly people who would greatly appreciate a moment of help.

Offer your hand to an older person who slowly walks across the street. Not only will that person be grateful for the physical support, but most likely, a moment of warm companionship will be enjoyed.

Find a home for a stray animal.

There are so many stray cats and dogs around, we barely notice them anymore. However, it is possible that you could easily find a home for one or two of them. Ask your friends and neighbors if they might not enjoy having a new pet. To your surprise, they might. There are also shelters for animals in different neighborhoods. Locate the closest animal shelter in your neighborhood, and see if they might help a stray animal you've found.

Feed the seagulls in the winter.

The beach is beautiful in winter. Dress warmly, and take a hot mug of coffee or hot chocolate and a bag of bread crumbs along. Go and feed the seagulls. They are hungry in winter and need all the food they can get.

When someone comes to visit, take out a picture you have of them, frame it, and leave it where they can see it.

Everyone loves to see pictures of themselves. If your guest sees that he or she is so important to you that you actually have a photo around, think how wonderful that person will feel knowing that he or she occupies a special place in your heart.

A little extra attention goes a long way. The extra time you spent framing a photo and placing it within your home will certainly make a difference. It will make a difference to you too. Leave the picture out after your guest has left, keeping the good feelings present in your mind.

Visit a shut-in and bring a little gift.

It is amazing how many of our senior citizens are living alone as shut-ins unable to get out by themselves. Call your local senior citizen center, meals-on-wheels organization, church, or temple and find out the identity of the shut-ins. See if you can pinpoint those people who would enjoy a visit.

Call the person and arrange a time for a visit. When you arrive, bring a little gift. You can bring a magazine, tape, bowl of soup, or any other lovely surprise. You can also ask if there is anything special the elderly person needs or wants.

Just a short amount of time on your part can mean a great deal to individuals in a situation like this. The shut-in person will not feel entirely forgotten. You will bring contact and refreshment from the outside world to that person. If it is at all possible, perhaps you can arrange some regular visits, so that person has something to look forward to.

Create a telephone tree for someone in need of help and support.

A telephone tree consists of a group of people who telephone an individual in need of support. Each person in the "tree" only has to make a call once a week, but the individual who is receiving the support has someone calling every day.

Some people for whom you might wish to create a telephone tree include those who are seriously ill, undergoing treatment, have lost a family member, or an individual in recovery from drug or alcohol addiction. Perhaps these individuals do not have a network of their own that can back up their daily effort to recover. Support like this can often make the difference between hope and despair, success and failure, even life and death, to many who are alone.

The greatest tragedy is indifference.
—THE RED CROSS

MARCH 1

Make a special romantic date with your wife, girlfriend, or significant other. Dine them, wine them, and let them know how important they are to you.

It's easy to take the most important people in our lives for granted by keeping to a routine. Take extra care to plan a special, romantic date for the one you care most about. Find a romantic restaurant, dance club, or jazz concert, or take a walk in nature or horse and buggy ride around the city. Dress up, bring a camera, bring flowers, order a delicious meal. Take time on this occasion to let the person know how important he or she is to you. You will both feel refreshed and renewed after this delightful outing, and most likely you will feel eager to plan the next one very soon.

MARCH 2

Don't honk your horn on the road today, even if you have a reason to do so.

It is so easy to get exasperated on the road. Other drivers can be careless and thoughtless. However, honking only increases tension, anxiety, and general noise. Control your use of the horn, which is intended to be used as a warning during times of danger only. Contribute to an atmosphere of patience and calm on the road, though others may be doing otherwise. Even a moment of quiet and clarity may prevent an accident.

**When someone who has been visiting you
leaves, walk them to their car. If that person is
not driving, walk him or her to the door.**

It is a special feeling to be accompanied during times
of arrival and departure. When we walk someone
right to their car or to the door, not only does that
person feel cared for, but the individual feels as though
we want to be with them up to the very last moment
and are grateful for the visit. This makes times of transition easier. The person who is leaving feels especially
appreciated and does not feel alone.

**When visiting a graveyard, put a flower or
some other token on a stranger's tomb.**

When we visit a graveyard to remember someone
who has been dear to us, many people leave a
flower or other token of remembrance behind.

If we stop and pay our respects to someone else who
has lived and loved and we leave a flower behind for
them, we are extending our capacity to be grateful for
all life. It is also possible that somewhere, somehow this
person's spirit will receive the gift so graciously left
behind.

At the supermarket, carry someone's bags to their car for them.

Often when shopping, we'll see someone old or infirm struggling with packages. It only takes a moment to help this person get his or her packages into the car. That extra help could mean a great deal.

Throw a surprise party for someone who has been particularly supportive of you.

Most of the time we do not notice or appreciate the thousands of tiny ways we are supported by family, friends, and even strangers. When we do notice it, we are reluctant to express thanks.

Choose someone who's been particularly supportive, and gather friends together to surprise him or her with a party. The party could be as small as three people or as large as one hundred. It could be as casual as your living room or as formal as a restaurant. Some might prefer something simple, like a picnic in their backyard.

Not only will this person be surprised and uplifted, but you and those who join together will experience unexpected delight.

Leave surprise notes of encouragement in hidden places.

Write a few notes of encouragement and put them in unexpected places, where the people for whom you are writing them will be likely to look. Some examples could be in a drawer, on their pillow, at their place at the table.

These little messages will surprise them and perk up their day.

At the end of every day, take a few minutes and write down everything that has happened that you feel good about. Call this your Book of Wins.

Our minds can become like dumpsters, filled only with what has not worked for us today. It is crucial to consciously reverse this focus.

Buy a small notebook and write Wins on it. At the end of the day, or when something happens, write down what occurred, or what you did that you feel good about.

Review the Wins of the day when you get a chance. You can also look back over past days and be amazed at how much has happened that you were pleased about. When your consciousness fills with successes, that produces more success for you. It will also make you a happier person and increases your chances of doing well.

Give someone with whom you are upset the benefit of the doubt.

It's so easy to blame others for disappointments we've had, and find ways of making them look like villains. This only serves to keep our anger alive. It also prevents full understanding of all the factors involved in our difficulty.

If you are thinking ill of someone, reverse this immediately, and give the person the benefit of the doubt. Find reasons to explain that behavior in a way that puts the individual in a positive light. This will make room for that person to save face and perhaps even apologize for some misunderstanding that began inadvertently.

Not only will doing so make your relationship stronger, but the atmosphere of acceptance you generate will feel wonderful.

Put positive notes of encouragement for yourself where you can see them.

As the day goes on, our mind becomes filled with problems, difficulties, complications, and resentments. It is easy to lose track of inspiring thoughts. It is vitally important to keep positive thoughts around where you can see them. This counteracts negativity, and is like vitamins for your spirit and soul.

Write down two or three inspiring thoughts on small index cards (in bright colors), and put them where you can see them during the day. When you glance at them, take time to actually stop and read them aloud as well.

Find a wonderful thing about your secretary, or person who helps you, and tell them.

It is easy to find faults with our helpers. Our mind often gravitates to what is wrong with a situation. We must stop and consciously turn this attitude around. Some are afraid that if they compliment someone for working well, that person will ask for a raise, make other demands, or gain leverage. The opposite is true. The person will be more devoted, and enjoy doing his or her work more.

List three things that are wonderful about your secretary or some other person who helps you at work. Some examples could be that he or she always comes to work on time, is sensitive to your needs, stays later when needed, and makes that extra effort. Make a habit of saying at least one positive thing once a week. You might enjoy this so much, you'll tell them once a day. Watch how their work improves! Watch how much you enjoy doing this, too.

Learn how to say thank you in other languages, so you can speak to a person in their native tongue.

It is tremendously delightful for a foreigner to hear a person say "thank you" to them in their native tongue. It makes them feel like others are conscious of and sympathetic to them in a way they didn't imagine before.

Learn to say thank you in Spanish, French, Japanese, or any other language you come into contact with regularity. It will form a wonderful link between you and these individuals. It will also help to expand your own understanding of people who have different backgrounds from you.

Human happiness comes from perfect harmony with others.

—Chuang Tzu

MARCH 13

Volunteer at your local school.

There are many ways you can help out at your local school. Call the administrative offices and ask what help they need. Some jobs that might be available include helping with sporting events, in the lunchroom, at recess, in the kindergarten, the orchestra, band, or even general clerical assistance. Even if you can only spare one afternoon, the time you give will be greatly appreciated. It will also help you become aware of the needs and life of the community.

MARCH 14

Think about how the memory of someone you loved can best be honored. Do something unique, in line with who they were.

The best way to recover and heal from loss is to truly integrate all of the goodness and lessons the life of the person you lost brought you. We all want a sense of continuity. We want to know that who that person was and what they gave is not lost forever.

Take some time to think carefully about the life of the person who has passed away and how they can be best honored for the way they lived. What was most important to them? What work did they leave unfinished? What mistakes did they make that you might like to see corrected?

Take some appropriate action on their behalf and dedicate it to them. The best memorial for another person is a life well lived, knowing his or her positive influence continues.

Create your own special days to be commemorated every year. Think of two or three days when especially meaningful things happened in your life and celebrate them.

We are all accustomed to celebrating universal holidays and times of particular religious importance. However, in each of our lives, there are days when something of great meaning happened to us. Why not create your own personal holidays? Why not stop to acknowledge and celebrate times when you had an experience of great significance, when you were outstanding, or understood something precious about life?

For each of us these times will be different. It is a fascinating process to think about those days in your life. Declare them as special anniversaries. Celebrate them with or without a person you love, in a way that feels fitting.

By giving time and recognition to these landmarks in our lives, we remind ourselves of what is important, and say thank you for it.

Promptly return all calls you receive and thank the person for calling.

This deceptively simple action has tremendous impact on others. People are so conscious and grateful when someone returns their calls promptly and does not leave them dangling, waiting and wondering if you will call back. Returning calls promptly says, "You are important to me. And I respect your time and feelings."

It is also nice to actually thank the person for calling you. Let the person know you appreciate his or her reaching out. Calling is difficult for many people, and this sensitive acknowledgment of the effort involved will help the person make that next call.

St. Patrick's Day

Honor the Irish. Attend a St. Patrick's Day Parade and bring a friend.

This is a day the Irish celebrate their culture and history. As a teen, St. Patrick was kidnapped by an Irish raiding party and forced into slavery. After six years, he escaped, made his way home, and soon after received a divine call to return to Ireland as a Christian missionary. He spent the rest of his life founding churches and ordaining clergymen.

The day is celebrated with a parade, dressing in green (the color of Ireland), wearing shamrocks, and enjoying parties through the afternoon and evening.

Attend and enjoy the festivities. Give support to the Irish and what has made them unique.

Be friendly to telemarketers.

Telemarketers can be very annoying, calling us at home or at work in the middle of our activities. However, this is their livelihood, and it is not easy for them to make all those calls.

Even if you have to hang up quickly, just take an extra moment to be courteous and friendly when they call. Thank them for their trouble. Imagine that you are in their shoes.

Take someone to the airport, or meet an arriving plane.

If at all possible, take someone you know who is flying to the airport today. For the traveler, it feels wonderful to have that extra support before taking a trip, especially before a flight.

The same is true when someone is arriving. Having someone waiting for you when you arrive makes a person feel that they are important to someone and not alone.

Think of someone you are holding a grudge against. Buy that person a small present and send it to them.

The last thing we want to do is give up our grudges, our sense of righteous indignation. Yet holding a grudge hurts the person who holds it much more than the one who is the target of our angry feelings.

Nothing works as quickly to remedy the situation as reversing our usual behavior. Buy a small gift for the person against whom you hold a grudge. Have the present wrapped beautifully and send it to them. You might include a simple note saying you were just thinking of them and wish them well.

By embarking upon a different course of behavior, we start a chain of different responses.

> *With gentleness overcome anger,*
> *with generosity overcome meanness*
> *with truth overcome deceit.*
>
> —BUDDHA

When you leave the movie theater, subway, train, bus, or plane today, make sure your seat is really clean.

Many of us litter automatically in movie theaters, trains, buses, and subways and then think nothing of it. We do not realize that someone else is going to come and sit down in our place.

Not only is it unpleasant to alight in a messy spot, but we are making extra work for someone who, sooner or later, will eventually have to clean up our mess.

It is an expression of thanks and thoughtfulness to make certain we leave a place that we have used fresh and clean for another.

Stop controlling others.

Some of us feel that the only way to be secure is to control everyone and everything around us. Not only is this impossible, but it creates additional tension and anxiety both for others and for ourselves. Too much control can even cause obstacles and impediments of all kinds in our lives.

Consciously decide today to let others be as they are. Find someone you usually control a lot and allow that person to be himself or herself. You will be amazed at how much more easily and enjoyably your day will go. You'll also be delighted at the new sense of friendliness the person will feel toward you.

This will feel so good you might even try to stop controlling yourself. Just relax and enjoy who you are.

Bring mail that belongs to someone else, but has come to your house, to their house right away.

Occasionally the post office will drop someone else's mail at your house. This could very well be an important letter, check, or bill. The individual could have been waiting for it for a long time.

It is easy to let misdelivered mail sit on our table by telling ourselves, "I'll return it tomorrow." Make sure you return the letter to its rightful owner right away. This is a tremendously important and thoughtful act on your part. Not only will it relieve the person involved, but it is a way of helping out and giving thanks to the post office.

Enjoy Easter celebrations. Paint beautiful Easter eggs for a youngster, and find one way to renew your life.

Easter falls on a Sunday between March 24 and April 24 (the first Sunday following Lent). It is a time of rebirth and renewal, filled with hope and the promise of newness. Christians believe it is the time of Christ's ascension.

Enjoy the celebrations. Paint beautiful Easter eggs and give them to a youngster as a special memento. Invite others to an Easter meal and cook dishes that are special to you.

Above all, choose one way in which you can renew your own life and fill it with more hopefulness.

Pay your worker or helper immediately after their service has been rendered to you.

Many of us cause others to wait for payment, often long after they have rendered a service to us. We do not take time to consider how much the payment may be needed. Perhaps the individual supports others and sorely needs the wages he or she has earned.

According to the Bible, it is considered a form of theft not to pay earned money right away. The money now belongs to the worker, and we are unjustly using or holding it. On top of that, we may be causing unfair anxiety or shame in the worker by eventually causing that person to ask or plead for wages that are rightfully his or hers.

Build a birdhouse. Give it as a gift.

Spring is just beginning and soon new birds will be back. It is extremely enjoyable to take some wood and build a birdhouse. Make some space in it to put bird seed, and a place for birds to stand and sing.

When it is completed, give it as a gift to a friend. Not only will your friend enjoy it, but it will delight the birds as well.

Take one step toward doing something you have wanted to do for a long time but have been putting off.

We all have some kind of project or activity we plan to do someday. For many of us, that future moment never comes. The project or activity simply remains a dream. When we think of actually getting started, we may not know how to begin, or it may seem overwhelming.

To take even one small step toward the realization of that project can have a tremendous impact. One small step leads to another. Just by doing something, we feel we have begun. The next steps seem less overwhelming.

Actually, if we do a little bit every day, the project develops a momentum of its own. Even five or ten minutes a day can have far-reaching effects.

Nobody could make a greater mistake
than he who did nothing
because he could only do a little.
—EDMUND BURKE

Think well of yourself. Find five things you've done this week that you can be proud of and write them down. Take it in. Feel good about yourself.

Most of us are tremendously hard on ourselves. Usually we think about what hasn't worked well in our lives and all we have left to do. We seldom give ourselves credit for our many accomplishments.

Sit down today and give yourself a chance to consider five things you can be proud of. This can be five things you've done, or five steps you've taken. Whatever they are, write them down. This will help you absorb them more fully.

Now, linger a little over each of them. Give yourself the approval you deserve. So often we desperately seek approval from others, but refuse to give it to ourselves. Once we start approving of ourselves, it is amazing how others begin approving as well.

On a date that isn't what you hoped it would be, find three good things about the person and focus on them.

Everyone, at one time or another, has found themselves on a date that wasn't everything they hoped it would be. Rather than be bored, sullen, petulant, or find things wrong, find three good things about the person you're with. Focus on those all night.

You'll be amazed at how interesting a boring evening can become if you take the time and effort to look a little more deeply at the person you are with. Everyone has something to offer. It's up to you to find out what.

If you have a skill that could help someone who is out of work get a job, teach it to him or her.

We do not realize how helpless someone can feel when they are out of work. Jobs in a person's field may be hard to get, or the market may be changing dramatically. Perhaps the skills he or she has used in the past are becoming outdated.

We may have a skill that another lacks. If someone you know is out of work, make a point of offering to teach him or her your skill, so that person can use it to get another job. The more skills he or she has the more possibilities are available. For all you know, this new skill could open many new doors. As the Bible says, there is no greater charity than enabling someone to earn a living.

As you walk down the street and see the meter at someone's car has run out, slip a quarter in. Give them extra time.

So many times our meter for parking runs out just a minute or two before we get back. Then we receive an expensive parking ticket that could have been avoided if we returned a moment or two earlier.

If you are walking by and happen to see a car parked at an expired meter, why not slip a quarter in and help that person avoid a ticket today?

Even though that person does not know who you are, he or she will feel touched and supported, as if the world contains unknown angels and friends.

Allow someone to feel really good about themselves vis-à-vis you. Show the person that he or she has made you happy.

It's extremely difficult for some of us to let others know that they've succeeded with us, made us happy, or fulfilled a need. We're afraid that if they know this, they'll have some power over us. So, we pretend their contributions haven't meant much. Some people let others feel that no matter what they do or give it's not good enough. This keeps the other person on the string, constantly striving to make someone happy and constantly unable to do so.

Turn this pattern around today. Allow someone to win with you. Let that individual see that you are happy, that a contribution has been made to your life. You can tell that person with words, with a smile, gesture, or note. In a sense, this action releases a person from further obligation and guilt. You are allowing the person to give because he or she wants to, not because the person is bound by an iron chain. Think how much better you'll feel in the future receiving offerings that come freely, and how much better he or she will feel giving that way.

APRIL 1
April Fool's Day

Today be a fool for love. Praise everyone you meet all day long.

The biggest surprise we can give someone is to completely accept that person just as he or she is. Usually, before we accept a person we want so many things about that person to be changed.

Today be a fool for love. Praise everyone you meet all day long. Find something real to praise them about and then go ahead and do it. At the end of the day, you'll be flying high, and so will everyone else.

APRIL 2

Think of some people who need help, include them in your thoughts, and if you pray or meditate, include them in your prayers.

Today think of a few people who need help and offer prayers, good thoughts, or meditations for them. Take a few moments to consciously send them light, healing, love, or comfort. Visualize their lives improving. Hold them in your heart. If you choose to, you can do this for short periods throughout the day.

Our inner relations toward others can have a profound effect. Some have claimed to be healed completely through the intervention of meditation and prayer. To send good will to another can only have a strengthening effect on both of you.

Offer to talk to or teach a class or one-time workshop at your local continuing education or senior citizen center.

We have so much to offer. By giving to others, we are forced to think about what it is that matters to us, what we have learned or accomplished in our lives, and to find a way of sharing it. You will be amazed at how much your personal knowledge or skills can mean to someone else.

Make a list of what you know, do, or care about that might be of interest to others. Prepare a short talk, class, or workshop about it and offer this knowledge at your local continuing education department, church, synagogue, senior citizen center, library or any other community center where classes are given.

Doing this will greatly expand your knowledge and your joy will be enhanced.

Return an object that you borrowed and have put off returning. When you return it, add a little gift.

Often we accumulate borrowed things, not thinking of the people who lent them to us. It can be awkward for the person who loaned it to have to ask for it back, and there's no reason why this person should have to do so. When you return an object you've borrowed for a while, as a way of saying thank you for the extra time, why not return it with a little gift? The gift can be simple, like stationery, candy, or any token of appreciation the person might enjoy. In this way, you are giving your friend a message that you are aware of the sacrifice on his or her part.

Practice patience today. When you feel hurried, restless, or pushy, stop, breathe, count to ten, and let things take their own course.

We live in a world of immediate gratification, where we expect to get what we want the minute we want it. Every day there is pressure to get where we're going twice as fast as we did yesterday. This takes a huge toll both on our nervous systems and on our enjoyment of life.

Today, when you find yourself hurried, pushed, or in a frenzy to get something done, slow down, and just decide not to push the river but to let it flow. Your patience will always be appreciated by another, and your own body will also be the beneficiary.

> *Why not just let the sun shine*
> *when it shines,*
> *Why not just let the rain fall*
> *when it rains.*
>
> —ZEN SAYING

Relinquish a destructive fantasy.

We all have fantasies of one kind or another that are destructive for us. Some of these may be concerning a negative relationship, or we may be holding onto a dream that will never come true and that stops us from moving ahead.

Pinpoint a fantasy (dream or behavior) you hold onto that is destructive for you. Write it down. Some examples would be the desire for revenge on someone, fantasizing about having an affair with someone else's wife or husband, dwelling on things you do not have that others do. Then, simply relinquish this for an hour or two. See how much better you feel.

It is easier to dismantle these destructive fantasies if we start by giving them up for an hour or two. For some, letting go will feel so good that they will not want to take them back at all. For others, the process will be gradual. The next day or week, you may decide to give up the fantasy for a little longer. In this way, you dilute the power that the destructive fantasy has over you.

Dedicate a plaque in someone's memory.

Dedicate a plaque at your local church, synagogue, or school in memory of someone who has passed away. You might also see if it is possible to dedicate a portion of a park.

This keeps the person's memory alive, honors his or her memory for all passersby to see. If you care to do so, write something special on the plaque as well. Some examples of what you could write might be: He gave where others give up; loving and giving with her heart and hands; alive in our memories; or a person such as this never fades away.

Honor Passover by giving thanks for the times you passed through trouble safely.

For the Jews, Passover is a holiday of redemption, of being saved from oppression, and seemingly insoluble obstacles by obeying the word of God. This holiday falls during the second week of April.

Matzoh (unyeasted, flat bread) is eaten in remembrance of the flight from Egypt, as there was no time to let the baked bread rise. Matzoh is also a symbol of a lack of pride and of humility.

How many times do we actually remember our times of trouble and give thanks for our safe passage? Once these times are over, it is easy to forget them and take our well-being for granted.

Give special thought to the times of trouble in your life, and see if you can recognize the assistance and support you received from a higher power.

APRIL 8

Buddha's Birthday

Spend some time in silence, in honor of the Buddha's birthday. Tell others about it.

The birthday of the Buddha is celebrated by Buddhists all over the world. The founder of one of the great religions of the East, the Buddha taught silent meditation, humility, and the need to be continually mindful of our thoughts, words, and deeds.

In Buddhist temples, a statue of the Buddha is decorated with flowers; water is poured over it as a symbol of the beauty, enlightenment, and purity of the Buddha's way of life.

Participate in this gentle pathway by being particularly mindful of your own thoughts, words, and deeds, and by experiencing the power and value of silence. This is a way of becoming sensitive to and respectful of all of life, thereby giving thanks for the entire creation.

> *Better than a hundred years of ignorance*
> *Is one day spent in reflection.*
>
> —BUDDHA

APRIL 9

On the weekend, call up a person whom you know is alone just to see how that person is doing.

The weekends are hard for those who are alone. This is the time when others are together and when the person who is alone has time to be aware of his or her life situation.

For many it is difficult to reach out and make friends. It is also difficult to ask for companionship. A call to someone just to say you are aware of that individual and care can make an entire day much brighter. Your call will make him or her feel less alone. It may also help that person reach out to others or take other positive steps.

If there is a child who has had a recent loss or difficulty in your youngster's class, see if you can include that child in your family outing.

Children in school who have suffered a loss or difficulty, such as divorce, often feel different from others, as if they don't belong. Their classmates may keep distant from these children as well for fear such a thing could happen to them, or because they don't know how to act with the child or children now.

If someone in your child's class has had such a loss, make a point of helping your youngster and this classmate to cope with it lovingly. Include this classmate in a family outing with your own child. Perhaps you can make a point of taking a few other children from the class along as well. Doing so can teach them all that loss is natural, that those who are grieving are no different from us, and that we have the ability to relate to and support people going through all aspects of life.

Buy or make little gifts for those you live with and hide them in a special place where they will be found.

Everyone loves surprises. Buy or make something simple that you know those at home would enjoy—cookies, a calendar, a new pen, a new book they've been interested in, a magazine about their special interest. Wrap the gift nicely and hide it in a place where they are likely to look, such as a drawer, on top of a pillow or a desk, or the place where they hang their coats.

What a lovely way to say you're special and I've been thinking of you.

APRIL 12

Take a long bubble bath.

Our body works so hard for us all day long. Many do not take the time to say thank you to it. They feel guilty about self-indulgence. But it is not self-indulgent to take good care of yourself. Your body will return the effort spent on its behalf many times over. A long bubble bath can be deeply relaxing and soothing. It can be a time for comfort and also quietly dwelling on what's important.

APRIL 13

Volunteer at your local police station to help remove graffiti.

So many of our public spaces are desecrated by graffiti of all kinds. Rather than pass by and do nothing, take responsibility for this space, and volunteer at your local police station to help remove graffiti on a public area, perhaps by painting over it or white-washing the wall.

If each of us took personal responsibility for our communal spaces, all our cities would be uplifted and thrive.

APRIL 14

Mail a small donation to a charity of your choice.

There are so many financial requests made of us, it can seem overwhelming. Many of us just shut down. We do not realize that even a small donation made to a charity of our choice counts a great deal. If we make this small donation regularly, before long it becomes a significant amount.

Decide on a small sum that you can easily afford, and send it to a charity of your choice. Try to do this regularly. See how good you will feel. Some charities you might look into include the Make a Wish Foundation (for children with terminal illnesses), the Red Cross, the Gay Men's Health Crisis (for AIDS), Unicef (United Nations Children's Fund). There are many, many worthy causes.

APRIL 15

Put up pictures of scenes that are uplifting to help you picture life as you would like it to be.

There are many ways to keep ourselves focused and uplifted. When reaching for a goal it is better to focus upon the solution than the problem.

Cut pictures out of magazines and newspapers of scenes that represent solutions for you. Paste them up where you can see them. In this way, you will envision the accomplishment of your goal and implant supportive visual images in your mind.

For example, if you would like a fine romantic relationship, cut out pictures of people who are happy together, laughing and smiling. If you would like a new home, cut out pictures resembling the kind of home you are dreaming of. This keeps the final goal alive in your mind and it lets you see that it is possible.

If you are going to visit a family with a new baby, bring a gift for the older child too.

It's always hard for an older child when a new baby arrives, receiving so much attention and so many gifts. The older child can easily feel forgotten and displaced. It is important to help this youngster remember that he or she is just as dear now as before.

You might bring a reading or coloring book, crayons, a puzzle, or some simple item that will tell the child that he or she has not been brushed aside.

Patronize a store or restaurant in your neighborhood that you have never been to before.

It is easy to get into a routine of patronizing the same stores and restaurants. They are familiar to us, and we feel comfortable knowing what to expect.

Give other merchants and restaurant owners your business as well. Step off the beaten path. Not only will you expand your horizons by meeting new individuals, tasting different kinds of food, and being exposed to other products, but those whom you patronize will receive additional support as well.

APRIL 18

Instead of just thanking a client for his or her business with words send a box of candy, fruit, nuts, or cigars.

It's easy to take established clients for granted. We provide them with a service and sometimes feel thats enough. Today, however, make a special point of thanking your clients for choosing you. Instead of just saying the words, go get a box of candy, cigars, or fruit and nuts for them—anything that they would enjoy. One action is worth a thousand words.

APRIL 19

Protect our endangered species.

There are many species of animals that are presently in danger of vanishing, such as the red wolf, the manatee, the Florida panther, the black-footed ferret, California condor, and many others. The National Wildlife Federation and the Sierra Club are two organizations dedicated to the work of saving them. They have educational programs as well as specific ways in which concerned individuals can be of help. Both organizations have local chapters near you.

Call a local chapter and find out more about the work they do. See how you can participate in leaving this earth and the creatures who live on it alive and well cared for.

The world is a womb, not a tomb,
A place where things are engendered,
And brought to life.

—HENRY MILLER

Help someone start a new project they can't do alone.

For some people, starting something new is very difficult. Once the project is underway it can be kept alive, but startup seems overwhelming.

If you know someone who has a project he or she can't start alone, offer your help. Sometimes it's just enough to know someone is on the team so he or she can check in with you from time to time.

Other people may need you to walk them through the early stages. Some may need you to actually help them gather information and resources.

By getting someone started in this manner, you give more than temporary support—you give a whole spectrum of new possibilities in that person's life.

Get tickets for a theater or movie. Surprise someone with them.

Although many friends of yours would enjoy seeing a play or a movie, they may not take the time and effort to get tickets and make arrangements themselves. Find out a time when you know a friend is free, make a date to spend time together, and then take it upon yourself to go get tickets for a play or movie that the person will enjoy. When the time comes to get together, surprise him or her with the tickets.

The time you spend at the performance will be enriched even more by the trouble you took to create this event.

Are you fun for your child to be with? If not, turn this around. Be a lot of fun for your child today.

Most of us are very concerned about how our children are behaving with us, but not so concerned about how we are coming across. Do we play the role of parent (relative or grandparent) too seriously? Are we always finding something wrong? Do we think our role consists of our teaching or disciplining the child? Does the child look forward to spending time with us?

Discover if you are fun for your child to be with. Would the child choose to be with you if he or she could? If not, turn this around. Be a lot of fun today for your child. Play. Be silly. Sing funny songs. Teach the child a dance you enjoy, or get a musical instrument you can play (even a toy one will do). Do art work together, take a walk and look at rocks. Feed the ducks, collect autumn leaves. There are thousands of things you could do to make your time together fun.

Most of all, be a person, not just a parent, and the child will appreciate it.

If a friend is having a problem, be there until the end.

It is easy to become exhausted by our friends' problems, especially if they call and tell us about them over and over again. After a while we grow hopeless, and do anything we can to get off the phone. We listen perfunctorily and offer superficial solutions. In a sense, we have given up on them.

Don't give up on a friend who is having a problem. Really stay there until the end. When the friend calls, really listen. You don't have to offer solutions, but you can sympathize with what they are going through.

Many times all that's needed is to know someone is there who truly cares. If a person really feels listened to by someone who believes in that person, that in itself helps him or her come up with workable solutions.

Wildlife Week

Become a land steward. Learn about and take care of wildlife preserves.

Both the National Wildlife Federation and the Sierra Club are committed to making certain that nature preserves will never be destroyed.

They have educational programs and recreational and service trips available. Service trips are a rewarding mixture of work and fellowship. Some service trips include hiking along beaches and cleaning them as you go, gathering on wooded farms to survey and clean out wood duck boxes, cutting sapling trees and shrubs to open up a field, and erecting bird boxes.

Days like these provide multiple benefits. You spend time outdoors, become closer to the world you live in, actively help in its upkeep, and have the pleasure of sharing this experience with new like-minded friends.

Why not enhance the entire adventure by bringing someone you care about along?

Create an outdoor art show of children's paintings.

Children create an abundance of wonderful paintings in school all year long. Go to a neighborhood school, ask for the best of these paintings, and honor and acknowledge these children by having an outdoor art show of their work in the spring.

Their work can be displayed in a park, on a block, a public square, or space that might house any craft show. The children and their parents will be delighted and others too will enjoy the exhibit. You will implicitly offer the message that the public values and appreciates children's art. What a boost for everybody.

During a stay in the hospital, bring candies or fruit for the nurses and staff.

Nurses and staff in the hospital have continual demands made upon them. Although they must constantly care for and nurture many, very few take the time to nurture them. Even when nurses and staff do their best, many patients, in pain and distress, are unable to thank them properly.

If you are in the hospital for a stay, have someone who is visiting bring candies or fruit not only for you, but also for the nurses and staff. This is a generous way of thanking them for their help and the work involved.

Don't be angry with someone you have a right to be angry with today.

We can have many justifiable reasons for being angry. Many people are insensitive. Others stimulate anger in us to feel powerful. Some do not feel they are alive unless they are angry at someone.

Whatever happened, give up anger today. Decide you will not let anger destroy the beauty of your day. No one has to live their life as a puppet, responding automatically with anger when someone pulls their strings.

Approach the person who angered you in a calm manner. Find soothing words to say. When we respond to anger with anger, the situation escalates. If we let go of our side of the rope, healthy emotions can arise.

Judge everyone favorably,
This promotes peace.

—Torah

Invite a few single men and women over for coffee and dessert.

Many of us know single men and women who are not dating or who are unattached, but we never consider introducing them to each other. We fear the two might not like one another and that it will have repercussions upon us.

Rather than setting up specific introductions, why not invite a group of singles you know over for coffee and dessert. You might even mix in a few couples. This way no one will feel on the spot, and yet all will have a chance to mingle and meet. Even if those attending don't become partners, it is always possible that they might become friends.

String rows of beads. Make each one unique. Give it to yourself and a friend.

It is simple, fun, and inexpensive to buy different beads and get an interesting string to put them on. The very act of stringing beads is soothing and can also unleash your creativity.

See if you can make each bead different on the strand. Some people like to paint their own beads; others like to draw little pictures on them. After the row of beads is strung, you can polish it, or even rub in a sweet-smelling oil.

Make one for yourself and then another for a friend. The person you give this to will have the double pleasure of having something unusual and the knowledge that it was handmade.

When you have to end a relationship, do it carefully. Leave the other feeling good about himself or herself.

For some, there is no greater hurt than to be rejected in a romantic relationship—even if there has only been one date. These kinds of wounds can take a long time to heal, leaving a person feeling insecure and unable to go forward and meet someone new.

If you have decided to end a romantic relationship (no matter how long it has gone on), be very careful about the way you do it. Protect the other person's feelings. Let them know that your decision to leave has to do with you, not with any failing in them. Let them know the ways you have valued them. This will enable the other to move forward more readily. It will also enable you to feel good about yourself as well.

Spend time planting a garden—include fresh herbs, vegetables, or something else you can eat. Share your harvest with a friend.

We say thank you to the earth by caring for it—tilling the soil, preparing it, planting beautiful flowers to enjoy and herbs and vegetables to eat. If you do not live in a place where you have your own garden, you can create one in a window box. Some communities have community gardens, where residents can grow flowers and organic vegetables.

The soil wants to bear fruit and give beautiful flowers. By working with it and allowing it to nourish us, we become more closely in tune with nature and the rhythms of the seasons. By cooking and eating vegetables we've grown, and by sharing them, we increase the ability of our planet to feed all its inhabitants.

Organize a block party.

Block parties used to be common—everyone cooked a dish, put it out on tables in the middle of the block, and enjoyed each other's food and company.

Today most people keep to themselves. Many barely know their neighbors. It would take very little to ask those on your block or in your apartment building if they would like to participate in an old-fashioned block party or a pot-luck gathering. You will probably be amazed at how delighted they will be. You will even be even more pleasantly surprised to find out about the people who have been living near you. At the end of such a gathering, all will feel less alone.

Create a beautiful memorial in your home for someone who passed away.

There are many ways in which we can absorb the loss, honor the departed, and celebrate the ways in which their lives inspired us.

You will find it very healing and uplifting to create your own memorial in your home. You can invite whomever you feel loved the person or was touched by that person's life. There are many creative ways to say thank you and honor a beloved who has passed.

If the person was an artist, writer, or did other creative work, you might like to have those works on display. If there was anything written about that person, this would be a perfect time to read it. Those attending might wish to speak out from their own hearts. You can choose music the departed enjoyed, or spend some time together in prayer or silence.

A personal memorial of this nature, in which we have injected our own selves, helps bring a sense of completion, recognizing that although the person is gone his or her life still pervades our own.

Take a piece of wood that is lying around and whittle it into a smooth shape. Give it as a gift.

There are so many scraps of wood to be found every-where—broken branches of trees and driftwood on the beach. Rather than just leave them lying around, pick up one that looks interesting to you, bring it home, take out a penknife, and carve and then sand the wood into an interesting shape. Not only is this endeavor relaxing, it is also fascinating to discover how something that is about to be thrown away can be turned into a small work of art.

When it is all done, wrap it with a ribbon and present it as a personal gift to someone who you think would appreciate it.

Bring a friend to a party to which you've been invited.

If you're going to a party and a friend of yours has no place to go that evening, phone the host and ask if you can invite a friend. Often the host will be delighted to have you bring a friend. (If for some reason the host doesn't want to do this, nothing was wasted except a call.)

If you can bring the extra person, not only will they be grateful, but your time at the party will be much richer for having shared it.

Plan a family reunion.

How many of us have family that we haven't seen for years—aunts, uncles, first and second cousins, who have drifted away with time?

Plan a family reunion to take place in a month or two in the future. Call everyone up, or send out notes and invite the entire group together for an afternoon or evening.

Others will be surprised and touched that someone has taken the trouble. You can plan a barbecue, a picnic, a brunch at a home, or an evening in a restaurant. How you do it is up to you. Certainly all will come away feeling supported and uplifted. You might even decide to have such gatherings regularly.

Mail a recipe you especially liked to someone else who would enjoy it.

Sometimes we have a meal with a dish that is especially delicious and nourishing. This time, take a little trouble to get the recipe. If you are eating at a restaurant, sometimes the waiter can get you the recipe. If you have the dish at a friend's home, the friend will most likely be willing to share the recipe with you.

Once you have the recipe, take the time to mail it to a friend.

Spend quality time alone with your mother. (If this is not possible, spend quality time with her on the phone.)

Rather than just give a customary gift to your mother or go out for lunch or dinner, make Mother's Day—the second Sunday in May—special for both of you.

Arrange for the two of you to spend quality time alone together. Ask her how she would like to spend it, if there is some place in particular she would like to go.

When together, find out more about what her life is like now. What does she presently want or need? Is there anything special she would like to tell you or ask you about yourself?

See if you can give her what she wants. Even if you cannot, just this precious time is giving her a great deal.

If your mother has passed away, spend some time recalling the wonderful gifts she gave you in her life. Thank her silently for them, realizing that the link between you can never go away.

Personally attend your child's or your friend's ball game, dance, music recital, play, or art or science exhibit.

We hardly realize how meaningful it is for children, and adults as well, to have others present to root for them. Sports practice takes long, precious hours, as does working in the arts and sciences. All our accomplishments have so much more meaning when they are seen and appreciated by someone who is close.

Go out of your way to attend your child's game, recital, play, or art or science exhibit, even if it means taking a little time off from work. The appreciation and closeness you will develop will be well worth it. You will also inspire your child to continue the wonderful efforts he or she has begun.

On the birthday of your child, send a note to your own parents telling them that now you realize what it means to be a parent and how grateful you are for their efforts on your behalf.

There is no way to know what our parents have done for us until we raise a child of our own. We can celebrate both the birth of our children and the birth of ourselves as parents. At a time like this, how lovely to remember and credit our own parents (despite the mistakes they may have made). How touched they will be to receive a note from you telling them what you have learned about being a parent from them and how grateful you are for their efforts. (If possible, try to be specific in your note, mentioning special ways they contributed to you becoming parents.)

Do not gossip. Do not speak ill of another or listen if someone else is gossiping.

This may seem like an inordinately difficult exercise. Some might say, "If I don't gossip and don't listen to gossip, that leaves out 95 percent of all conversation." If that's true, perhaps it's time to find other ways of communication.

What may seem like harmless gossip actually has profound effects on everyone. A person's reputation can be easily damaged by gossip, effecting his or her ability to make a living or the establishment of the social contacts he or she needs. Words travel in strange ways. Even by listening to gossip you are participating in character assassination. (If no one listened, no one would speak.) As we all know, the tongue is mightier than the sword. Don't use your tongue to do harm.

Not participating in gossip will have profound effects on you and all your relationships. Trust in others will develop. You will feel more joy and well-being. Cynicism will diminish. Try it.

Be mindful of general noise that may disturb family and neighbors early in the morning or late at night.

Offer a few hours to help the mother of a newborn so she can have time to herself.

By being insensitive to the noise we make, we are often unaware how much of a disturbance we create for family and neighbors. If you get up early and leave the house while others are still sleeping, be mindful not to slam doors, rev your car in the driveway, or turn the radio up loud.

At night, when others might be sleeping, be conscious of how loud your TV or stero is playing, and if you are having a party, how much noise your guests make late at night.

Noise pollution can be as toxic as air pollution, especially if someone is sick or elderly. This extra awareness of others is an important way of showing those you live with that their needs are meaningful to you.

If you want to find joy. Do joy.
If you want to find peace. Do peace.

—TORAH

It is enormously time-consuming to care for a brand-new baby. New mothers sometimes become depressed after birth, when all their free time has suddenly disappeared. Even if you aren't caring for an older child, a new baby can consume every moment.

If you know the mother of a newborn, offer her some of your time to help with the baby so she can have an hour or two to herself. She might use the time to take a shower, read a book, or run out for a manicure. Even a little break can make all the difference to the mother in the first months of a new child's life.

MAY 13

Take a walk in your favorite place and thoroughly enjoy both the scenery and your own company.

Many of us feel we cannot enjoy outings unless we are with a special person to share the experience. Today, realize you are that special person and can thoroughly appreciate and enjoy a place by yourself.

Go to the seashore, a park, a special place in the country, or a neighborhood in the city where you feel particularly alive. Spend time there, walk around, take in the sights and smells, and realize what good company you are to yourself.

There is a great freedom in knowing and being your own best friend.

MAY 14

Hold the elevator door for others on their way in.

So often we see others running to catch an elevator just as the doors are about to close. It only takes a moment for someone in the elevator to reach out and hold the button, keeping the door open until everyone enters.

If you are in the elevator and notice someone about to get in, make sure you hold the door open for them. That person will greatly appreciate it.

MAY 15

Take a child, friend, parent, husband, wife, or significant other to public gardens in your neighborhood.

Many communities have public gardens where all kinds of vegetation thrive. There are beautiful walks to take there, and often employees can describe the flora and fauna for you in detail. Sometimes in the spring there are public events such as concerts.

Obtain the schedule of events, when they are open, lectures, if any, and go enjoy. Not only will the trip widen your vista of knowledge, but it will keep you in touch with nature.

MAY 16

When at a wedding, make the bride and groom happy. Find a way to make them laugh.

A Jewish custom offers a special blessing to make a bride and groom laugh and rejoice at their wedding. Guests dance and sing for the new couple. Sometimes they even wear funny masks and costumes. This blessing helps the couple and all those present, including the family, focus on the joy of the new union, rather than dwell on any feelings of tension or loss.

Just as you are about to say something in anger, hold your tongue.

It's very easy to let a moment's anger get the better of us and say something we will later regret. However, once words are spoken, they can never be taken back.

Count to ten. Bite your lips hard. Do anything you can until the angry moment passes. You can then consider calmly what to say. Whatever you say now will be much more thoughtful and bring much better results.

Collect a group of significant photos, articles, or mementos of a person's life, make a collage, have it framed, and give it to them— perhaps for an important birthday.

So many of us forget the phases of our lives, our accomplishments in them, the special moments we have lived through. It is an incredible gift to another to gather photos and all kinds of mementos describing their life, such as wedding invitations, graduation notices, trophies, awards, letters from old friends. Together these items portray many wonderful happenings that may now be in the background.

The person will be overwhelmed by your thoughtfulness and deeply touched by the memories you rekindle. This is a particularly wonderful gift for a significant birthday, but it can be given for any occasion or for no occasion at all.

Build a vegetable garden for people in need.

There are many people across our country who are poor, elderly, and in need of support and sustenance in any form. The Home Gardening Project Foundation was created by Dan Barker, who has devoted his life since 1984 to building free raised-bed vegetable gardens for people in need. This foundation is supported by government grants.

Most of the people for whom he builds the gardens are elderly or destitute. Not only does the garden provide approximately five hundred dollars worth of food each year, it gives its owners important work keeping it up, and it beautifies the neighborhood.

To learn how to build these gardens for others, or to set up a chapter of this foundation in your area, contact the Home Gardening Project Foundation in Jacksonville, Oregon. Not only will you support and nourish others in need, but you will find much satisfaction in this labor of love.

On a date, don't look at others, and don't talk about your past conquests. Be respectful of your date's feelings.

Some feel that the best way to impress a potential girlfriend or boyfriend is to brag about past conquests. They think this makes them seem more desirable, and gives the date the message that he or she has alot to live up to.

In most cases, this behavior has the opposite effect. It can cause insecurity in the other person, making that person feel competitive and less important.

When someone is granting you their time and feelings on a date, handle it carefully and with respect. This is an important way of thanking that person for being with you, whether you want to see them again or not.

An emotion which is overpowering
one moment, and gone the next,
cannot be called love.

—KABIR

MAY 21

Before you automatically say no to people, take time to consider if it is at all possible for you to meet their request. If you can, say yes instead.

Some of us are naysayers. We automatically reject and refuse many requests that come to us. At times, this is appropriate, but at other times, we are being rigid and stubborn. We could just as well say yes. (Or, if not yes completely, then perhaps we could find a compromise and offer an alternate response.)

When we tend to say yes, we embark on an adventure of opening new doors, meeting new people, giving to others, and discovering new things in life for ourselves.

MAY 22

As a guest, find three ways to help your host. Do them silently.

When we are a guest in someone's home, it becomes easy to see the little things we could do to be of help. We see what the host is giving us, and also what they might need in return.

Find three ways to help your host and do them silently. They could be little things, such as putting in lightbulbs, doing dishes, going to the market and bringing back some groceries, mowing the lawn, or perhaps a small repair you could do easily.

Your quiet thoughtfulness will be felt and appreciated. Additionally, you will feel better about receiving that person's hospitality if you can do your share.

Make or buy yourself your favorite meal.

We all have special, favorite foods that make us feel particularly nourished and loved. Some of us have these meals on a regular basis—others only once in a long while. When we give ourselves these kinds of meals, we do not feel so deprived.

Take the time to get the ingredients of the meal you like best, cook it for yourself, and serve it beautifully (perhaps by candlelight or with a flower or two). Now, sit down and, without rushing, enjoy it to the utmost. (If you are dieting and fear that this kind of food is not in your best interest, give it to yourself in the most appropriate form. Make it lowfat, or substitute ingredients that might be better for you. Find other ways to spice it up, so it still meets that special need.)

Or, if you prefer, take yourself out to a fancy restaurant.

Inspire others. Don't tell people all the reasons they can't succeed.

It's very easy to find problems, obstacles, and reasons why a person can't do what he or she has set out to do. The moment someone brings up a plan or desire, some of us start showering that person with bad news.

Today, make sure you speak only words of inspiration regarding anything someone else is planning to do, even something as simple as a party, an outing, or cooking a new meal. Tell them you know it will be wonderful and that you're looking forward to hearing how it turned out.

A few words of encouragement from another can make all the difference in whether another person feels confident enough to even start. Turn your words into vitamins and minerals for the soul.

Prepare a treasure chest for a woman you know who is getting married.

A treasure chest is an old-fashioned and delightful way to start a bride on her new life. It is actually a chest filled with personal touches, brimming with love.

You can buy an old chest and hand paint it. You could even paint on flowers or fruit or some other embellishment if you wish. Line the chest with lace or silk, and slowly collect personal items that will be meaningful to the bride. Sprinkle the items with potpourri or lovely smelling sachet. Some items could include lingerie, jewelry, little books of love poems, cards, recipes, photos of her as a child, old candlesticks—anything that enhances her sense of femininity and warmth.

The chest can be filled a little at a time. Not only will you enjoy doing this but the bride will be overwhelmed when the time comes for you to give it to her.

Give someone your seat on the subway, bus, or train.

When we are traveling in crowded trains, buses, and subways, it is easy to overlook someone who is older, pregnant, or otherwise more in need of a seat than you are. Look around and see who is standing. If there is someone who needs assistance, get up and offer that person your seat.

Go hiking today in a state park or some other environmental preserve.

It's important to take breaks from our routine activities, go outdoors, and appreciate the wonderful earth. Locate a large state park (preferably one you haven't been to before) or other environmental preserve with hiking trails. These trails allow you to enjoy and appreciate beautiful vistas you haven't seen.

A good hike not only provides excellent exercise, it puts you directly in touch with nature and with yourself in a way you may not have been before. This is a wonderful way of releasing tension and coming home refreshed and renewed.

Don't be so serious. Go to an amusement park with a child, a friend, a wife, husband, or parent. If no one is available, go yourself.

Usually we take ourselves and our lives so seriously, worrying about every little thing. It is crucial to know how to be in touch with our wonderful inner child. When this inner child is attended to, he or she brings joy and creativity into our everyday lives.

Being healthy means knowing how to play, be silly, and have a good time. It also means being able to let your hair down and not appear so important all the time.

An amusement park exists for people of all ages. Take yourself, a child, friend, wife, husband, or acquaintance to an amusement park for the day. Enjoy the sights and sounds. Watch the children having fun. Go on the rides that make you laugh. Buy yourself a hot dog and popcorn. Forget your cares and just have a good time.

Spend time at the planetarium learning all about the moon and stars.

We live a world of vastness, although our own point of reference can be very small. It is wonderful to take time to open our eyes to the incredible universe we are living in. A planetarium gives us a chance to look at and learn about the stars, moon, skies, and all the planets. It can be a dizzying experience to get a new view of our place in this world. We will return home humbled, excited, or feeling a new reverence for the universe we are privileged to live in.

Go to your local Memorial Day Parade. Honor those who fell while fighting for their nation.

This is a day of special remembrance for those who lost their lives in honor of their nation. Parades and ceremonies are held throughout the country.

Make it a point of spending some time today attending a parade or event. Think about the lives of those who fought and died for this nation. Speak of it to others and offer your own prayer for them.

Not only will your presence and support be meaningful to the families of those remembered, but you will also gain a fuller appreciation of what these individuals sacrificed and left behind for you. This is also a good time to think about what kind of offering you can make to your nation as well.

If you are considering buying a pet, go to an animal adoption center instead.

There are so many delightful animals that have no home and are waiting at adoption centers. Many of these will be put to sleep if no one comes to claim them.

If you are looking for a pet, visit one of these centers and become acquainted with the animals there. Very likely one of them will claim your heart, and you will not only have a fine pet, but will have saved a life as well.

Find an entirely different way to celebrate someone's birthday.

We all get stuck in ruts. Although we feel safe doing what is familiar, if we stay on the same route indefinitely, our world can become narrow and small.

Find an entirely new way to celebrate someone's birthday. Decide to introduce that person to something he or she has never seen or done before. Open up the world for that person.

Some examples: Take them on a boat ride around the city; go to a completely new section of town; get a ticket for a long train ride to a new place; buy two tickets to the opera. The possibilities are endless. Let this day be a true adventure for both of you.

Go dancing with your spouse or friend.

Dancing is a wonderful way to rejoice in life, get exercise, be with others, enjoy music, and feel young and alive. Dancing with someone is also a terrific way to work out any tension in your relationship. You have so much fun together that, by the end of the evening, tensions disappear by themselves.

There are all kinds of ballroom, swing, square, and line dancing classes and places to go all week long.

If you are not an experienced dancer and feel awkward, see if you can join a class, or, perhaps at first you might just enjoy watching others.

After you are comfortable at a place, there's always room on the dance floor for you to join in as well.

Share your friends or business contacts.

Some horde their possessions and also their friends. They are afraid of allowing anything to get in the way of their relationship. But friends are for sharing. Good will always spills over to all.

See if some of your friends or business acquaintances who do not know each other would enjoy meeting one another. First tell them about each other and then invite both of them along next time you get together. Before you know it, the favor will be returned. You'll soon be meeting more friends as well.

What we give returns to us. When we are generous with our personal or business friends and possessions, we soon realize that we live in an abundant world where there is more than enough for everyone. We do not have to cling to our friends and possessions so tightly, fearing we'll lose the little we have.

If you see someone carrying packages that are heavy, stop and offer a hand.

We usually pass people by on the street without stopping to notice if they need a hand. If you notice someone carrying packages from the supermarket or from any other place that seem too heavy, offer a hand. Help that person carry a package or two. This will only take a moment of your time, but you will leave behind the feeling that burdens do not have to be carried alone.

Thank your child for coming into your life and all the love he or she gives you.

We take it for granted that our children should love us; we expect good behavior and expressions of gratitude from the time they are little.

How often do we realize all that the children are giving us? How often do we tell them so? Most children love and trust unconditionally. Unless we have pulled the rug out from under them, they look up to us, copy us, and strive to become like us as adults. Our children always want us to be the very best in all ways.

Stop and acknowledge how much your children give you. Thank them for coming into your life. Let them know how much they mean to you. Children need to hear this as much as adults. If you do this and mean it, honestly and regularly, your children will thrive.

JUNE 6

Take some underprivileged children for an outing in the country.

There are many poor children in the inner cities who do not have the luxury of even one summer day in the country. A day like this could mean a tremendous amount to such a child.

Look up the phone numbers for a child care center in an inner-city neighborhood near where you live. Find out the protocol for taking a few children on an outing in the country for the day.

There are many things you could plan for the day, like visiting a state park and having a picnic, hiking, or just letting the children play some games out in the fresh air.

If you cannot actually do this yourself, contact an organization such as the Fresh Air Fund, which sends inner-city children to camp free for two weeks each summer. Find a way to contribute to it.

JUNE 7

Be the first to say hello.

It is easy to wait to be greeted and feel overlooked by people who pass you by. Today give to others what you want for yourself. Be the first to say hello. Extend a handshake, smile, or friendly greeting. You will be surprised at how pleased the other person will be. Feelings of rejection will vanish as you realize that most of the time others are waiting to be greeted, just as you are.

Write a speech about someone's accomplishments and how they have inspired you, and deliver it at a gathering in that person's honor.

We all know someone whose accomplishments have inspired us. Not only do we rarely tell that person so, but how often do we stop and truly think of all the ways his or her achievements and the inspiration they have brought has affected our lives?

Sit down today and write a speech about someone in your life. Discuss the ways in which this person's accomplishments have uplifted your life. Create a gathering in that person's honor (a small party at your home will do) and, at the party, read your speech aloud.

Not only will it deeply affect the person you are honoring, but it will be a source of enlightenment for others as well. As far as you are concerned, you will have begun to give back to that person in some measure what he or she has given you.

Take someone to a museum you've never gone to before.

There are all kinds of museums where we can learn a great deal and have a fascinating day—art, science, historical, natural history, or religious. When we enter them, we leave our usual world behind and become exposed to new things. Who knows what kind of new ideas and inspiration you will bring back home?

If there is not a museum you haven't been to in your community, revisit one you have attended. You probably will find a brand-new exhibit just waiting for you.

As well as sharing quality time with your companion, the horizons for both of you will be expanded.

**Tell your wife, husband, or significant other
all the things they are doing right.**

Usually, we are focused on what is not working in a relationship, that which we want to improve or change. We spend endless hours thinking of ways to get the other to improve so we can feel more at ease. It is only rarely that we dwell upon all the things they are doing right.

Tell your wife, husband, or significant other all the things they are doing right. Take time out to do this. Sit down with them and make a point of letting them know how much that it means to you. They will be startled and delighted. Not only that, you will notice more and more "right" things start to happen spontaneously in your relationship. What we pay attention to increases, and little annoyances soon fall away by themselves.

**Personalize stationery with someone's name
on it and give a pack to him or her.**

When you are in the stationers, pick out a pack of paper or notes and print the name of a friend on it. The next time you see that person, give it to him or her. Not only will he or she enjoy having personalized stationery, but that person will be aware and grateful for the special time and thoughtfulness you invested in having it made.

JUNE 12

Make sure you have some fresh flowers near you today. Look at them often. Appreciate them.

Flowers give us love and pleasure just by virtue of what they are. When you have fresh flowers near you, your spirit cannot help but be lifted. You are also telling yourself you deserve this pleasure, and reminding yourself of the simple beauty available in life.

Keep fresh flowers near you. Look at them often. Allow yourself to be refreshed.

JUNE 13

Gather books from your home that you are no longer reading, and donate them to the library.

Over the years we collect many books that stay on our bookshelves long after we've stopped referring to them. These books might very well be enjoyed and used by others.

Gather the books together and bring them to your local library. (If you have children's books, there might also be reading rooms in the children's sections of hospitals that would be grateful for them.)

Books can have long lives of their own, and there are many individuals who will enjoy them long after you are finished with them.

If you are right in a dispute, give up being right and let the other person keep his or her pride.

For some of us, our entire lives revolve around being right. If we feel we have been wronged or are in a dispute, we will fight to the last inch to maintain our position—no matter the consequences. Sometimes we will continue to do this, even though it very well may cost us a precious relationship.

Why not see how it feels to let this pattern go just once. Even if you are right, give up being right. Let the other person win the argument, and save his or her pride. Harmony between two people—is more important.

What price do you pay for being right all the time? When another wins, so do you.

Generosity is the state of mind where
we accept another just as they are.

—Trungpa

Spend a day with your father at his place of work.

As a Father's Day celebration, and as a way to get closer to your father and know more about his daily life, spend a day with him at his place of work. Tell your father ahead of time that you wish to do this and schedule it in advance.

There are few better gifts than sharing a person's daily routines, efforts, trials, and rewards. Your father will feel touched that you want to know him better and go through his day with him. You will also enjoy the day immensely and find out new things about your father. The effects of a day like this linger long after the day is done.

Father's Day is celebrated on the third Sunday in June.

If you get a particularly good deal on a TV, car, radio, or any purchase that is important, let others know about it too.

Sometimes we get really good deals on a purchase that can be expensive, or we hear about something such as a discount auction, flea market, garage, or antique sale. When this happens to you, why not share the information with others you know?

Be conscious of and sensitive to the dietary needs of others.

It's amazing how unaware we are of the dietary needs and problems of others. Often we push all kinds of foods and drinks onto them that they may be working hard to resist.

Don't give fattening foods to someone who is dieting, or press alcohol on someone who has a problem with liquor. If you are having a guest and that person is vegetarian, kosher, or has other special food needs, be sure you have something he or she can consume.

When you are having a gathering or planning to go out to a restaurant, take a moment to ask the people if they have any special needs or desires regarding the kind of food they can eat. It is always possible to choose a restaurant or menu that is satisfying for everyone.

JUNE 17

Bring a child or friend to an aquarium.

We think that we are the center of the world, but there's an entire world in our oceans and rivers. It is fascinating to become acquainted with fish and reptile life of all kinds. There are even mammals in the oceans—like dolphins—that communicate and can be our friends.

Take some time to discover and appreciate all the wondrous life forms that occupy our world. Bringing a child or friend will open his or her eyes too.

JUNE 18

Give a gift subscription to a magazine in a subject that interests your friend.

If a friend or acquaintance has a special interest, why not give a subscription to a magazine that covers it. There are magazines on cooking, home repair, stamp collecting, architecture, writing—the topics available are endless. The magazine will come every month. Not only will the person have continuous pleasure and information from it, but each time it arrives he or she will feel especially cared for by you.

Spend time making puppets with a child. Help the child put on a puppet show.

Puppets are easy for children to make. They are also a wonderful way for youngsters to role play, and evoke what is going on in their lives. In Japan, puppet shows are as popular as theater is here.

You can make hand puppets or puppets with strings. Use odds and ends, and tie together scraps of cloth for the puppet's clothes. A child might enjoy painting faces on the puppets too.

Once the puppets are complete, invite a few of the child's friends or family over to see them, and have the child put on a puppet show.

The child will have the puppets say out loud and act out what he or she is feeling inside. Everyone will have a good time. A child's puppet show also serves as therapy for a youngster experiencing a difficult time who has trouble talking about it.

When you pass someone on the street who is troubled, stop a moment and say a silent prayer for him or her.

Most of us are overwhelmed by the enormity of suffering we see all around. When we pass a troubled person on the street, we turn away and leave as fast as we can.

If you see someone troubled on the street today, stop what you're doing and say a silent prayer for that person.

Some say they can feel the prayers of others and are uplifted by them. Others believe all prayers are answered.

*Everyone is the Temple
of the Living God.*
—Torah

JUNE 21

Summer Solstice

To celebrate the beginning of summer go to an outdoor concert in the park. Bring someone.

The summer is filled with all kinds of activities that are both inexpensive and enjoyable. In the warm weather, it is delightful to spend time outdoors. Summer can also be a time to take in new experiences, perhaps a concert you haven't heard before.

Celebrate the beginning of summer by taking a child, spouse, or a friend to an outdoor concert in the park. Call up your local park district and find out about any scheduled concerts. Make a point of attending one.

JUNE 22

At dinner with the family, engage in conversation. Don't read, watch TV, or listen to the radio. If you don't normally do so, make an effort to attend your family dinner tonight.

It is easy to avoid spending quality time with those with whom we live and care about the most. After a long day at work, many relax at dinner by watching TV, reading the paper, or listening to the radio. But dinner can be one of the rare times when the entire family is gathered. This is a perfect opportunity to find out about each other's days, and offer support and consideration.

Quality time spent each day with your family is precious and builds the basis for relationships that endure through time. Once each youngster is grown and out of the house, this opportunity cannot be recaptured.

If an older parent or relative becomes ill, take time to nurse him or her yourself.

It is very easy and common these days to send an older parent or relative away to be cared for—or to hire others to do the physical work that is entailed at home. However, a large part of caring for another is the love expressed in handling their needs. Being touched and handled by someone you are close to lifts one's spirits and preserves dignity.

If it is at all possible, directly participate in the nursing care of your older, infirm parent or relative. This close, physical contact will say more to them than a thousand words. It will also give you an opportunity to give something back for the years of care you received, heal any old wounds, share precious moments, and in general feel better about that person's aging and illness, and your possible loss.

If it is not possible to keep this person at home, see if you can join in his or her physical care for some portion of time at the nursing home. The intimacy the two of you share will resonate with you the rest of your life.

Go roller blading with someone you like or by yourself.

Roller skating and roller blading are both wonderful exercise and a good time. Take a friend or a child with you to a skating rink. Spend time together roller skating. Or, if you can do it, roller blade together in the street. Enjoy the new view of life you have as you are whirling along.

Give the right of way to a pedestrian who is crossing.

Some of us are demons in our cars. We let out all of our aggression and competitiveness when we are hidden behind the steering wheel. If someone is crossing the street when we want to make a turn, we resent holding back and letting that person go.

Watch yourself in your car today. When a pedestrian is crossing, wait patiently. If they happen to look up at you, you might even smile.

Courtesy on the road is always appreciated. It is sadly absent these days. And hostility—even something as minor as cutting someone off—can escalate to something much worse.

Be a Big Brother or Big Sister to a child.

There are numerous children lacking in guidance, friendship, and time with adults. These children desperately need role models. Big Brothers and Big Sisters are organizations that arrange for you to spend a certain amount of time each week with such a child. There are many things you can do with the child, such as playing ball, taking walks, going over homework, or hearing about what's going on in their lives. Whatever you do, the most significant part for the child is to finally know someone cares. The little time you spend can make a significant impact on this youngster's entire life.

When you see someone handing out flyers on the street, take one, look at it, and really thank them for their trouble.

We all tend to brush people off, especially people on the street handing out flyers. This kind of reaction makes the person feel insignificant, as if what they are doing doesn't matter at all.

Whatever work a person does makes a difference to him. He or she is making an effort, has needs and feelings, and is contributing whatever he or she has to contribute.

When you see someone handing out flyers today, stop, take one, look at it, and ask a question or two about it if you can. Really thank the person for giving it to you. This will make an enormous difference to the individual, who will feel as if what he or she is doing matters to someone.

Write a letter to an old friend you haven't seen for a long time.

There are many old friends in your past that you're letting drift away. Why not stop and remember who they were to you? Take a few moments and reconnect. Fill them in about what has happened in your life. Find out how they are. You might even want to go to the nearest card shop and send a friendship card.

They will be delighted to hear from you. You will be delighted with the renewed friendship too.

Have a garage sale of objects you don't need or want in your home and offer the proceeds to a charity.

Go through your home and collect everything you no longer need or use that could have some value to another. Put the objects in your garage to be priced and labeled. Then, announce a garage sale.

Take the proceeds from this sale and offer part—or all—of it to a charity of your choice. Not only will your house feel less cluttered, but you will be helping others in need.

Property given away is the only kind that will be yours forever.
—MARTIAL

Publicly credit those who have contributed to your achievements.

So often we overlook the fact that many of our accomplishments not only are due to our own efforts, but to the input others have had. If someone has made a contribution to something you have done, credit that person publicly. Not only will doing so mean a great deal to the person, but it is only fair. For instance, if you receive a public honor, as you accept it, mention those who have contributed to your achievement. If you excel in a sport or an art, take time to credit your coaches and teachers. Even if you have baked a wonderful cake and others are enjoying it, if the person who gave you the recipe is present, mention that as well.

If we look closely, we will see that all our achievements and delights have been the result of many people's input. Let them know. Give them thanks.

JULY 1

Make sure your pet does not annoy your neighbors.

Pets can be a wonderful source of companionship and pleasure. However, some of us have pets that bark all day, run away, jump on visitors, go into the neighbors' garbage, or mess up the neighbors' lawn. Our neighbors may feel uncomfortable saying anything to us about it and suffer silently.

Be aware and take responsibility for your pet's actions. If the pet requires training, do not hesitate to take it for a few classes to correct disturbing behavior. Not only will you be helping your neighbor feel better, but proper behavior is also good for the pet.

JULY 2

Take a friend to the circus or rodeo.

Take a friend, child, parent, spouse, or anyone at all to the circus or rodeo. It will give you all an upbeat, fun time together, time to laugh, see circus artists, animal acts, and feats you can't see anywhere else.

JULY 3

Patronize a local craft or antique fair.

Craft and antique fairs are always going on. These are places where individuals come and exhibit the work they've done themselves. It is lovely to take time to go to them, and acknowledge the efforts of these individuals. It took time and care to make the crafts on display. They are a direct expression of each individual's self.

Even if you don't buy something, you will meet new people, and support their efforts just by attending. You can also support the craftsmen by telling them how much you appreciate their work.

There are all kinds of hand-crafting activities you might not have been exposed to before. Perhaps one will strike your fancy, and you'll be an exhibitor yourself a year or two from now.

JULY 4
Independence Day

Have a barbecue for all your friends to celebrate Independence Day.

On this day when Americans gather to celebrate the country they live in, have a barbecue and invite as many people as you can. If you don't live in a house, organize a picnic in a local park and see that all are welcome.

This is also a good opportunity to get to know neighbors and create a good sense of community for all.

JULY 5

Have a paint-date with a child.

Buy some canvases, sketch pads, paints, and paint brushes, and invite a child over for a paint-date. Spread out the materials for both of you and spend time painting together. Let yourself be as creative as you like. This is your time to be a child too. Admire the child's work and let him or her admire yours as well. Talk about what you both are doing. It will be tremendous fun, and you will realize that there is a great deal you can learn from the child. Let the child know it, too. Thank the youngster for all that he or she contributes.

Children learn best while doing an activity they love with an adult. If the adult is enjoying it as well, it enhances the experience greatly. The precious hours spent together remain in their memory a long time, and the activity itself retains a special feeling for them.

JULY 6

Adopt a highway or adopt a street.

The Adopt a Highway–Adopt a Street program allows corporations and individuals to take responsibility for keeping the sides of their highways and streets clean. Organizations or individuals can sponsor a length of highway (a mile in some states, two miles in others). They pay a specified amount each month and those affiliated with the program make certain their stretch of highway or street is kept clean. In return, the name of the organization and its logo is put up on a sign along the side of the highway or on the street.

In the Adopt a Street program, the individuals or corporations sponsoring it can do the cleaning themselves, if they wish. Call the Adopt a Highway office in your area for detailed information.

> *Our work lies in that which is simple,*
> *Yet we seek that which is difficult.*
> —MENCIUS

JULY 7

Take a child to a lake to go out in a rowboat or canoe.

It is peaceful and beautiful to go rowing or canoeing on a lake. We feel close to the water, the sky, the sunshine, and each other. The rhythmic feeling of the water on the boat helps many relax, smile, and be who they are.

Find a park where rowboats or canoes are rented (if you don't have one of your own), and invite a child or special friend with you for the afternoon. The day will bring you closer to yourself and each other.

JULY 8

Don't go to bed angry at someone in your family or anyone else. Talk things out.

When we go to bed angry, not only is our sleep disturbed, we wake up the next day with heavy emotional baggage. Once we get into this kind of pattern, the anger can fester for a long time. With each passing day, the original situation that caused the problem becomes blown out of proportion.

If someone or something has angered you during the day, make it a habit to get it resolved before you go to bed at night. Talk it out with the person. Tell him or her you don't want to go to bed angry. Even if the situation cannot be fully worked out, make up with each other. It will be much easier to find solutions the next day when the anger is gone.

Don't complain about your misfortunes. Be an inspiration to others.

A wonderful gift you can give to the world is to not complain about your misfortunes. Everyone has difficulties they deal with. People do not wish to hear more troubles, but would like to hear words of inspiration.

No matter what you are going through, when people ask how you are, find something good to say. Focus on anything you feel good about, a success at work, the health of your children, a letter you received from an old friend, the enjoyment of a sport, or the fact that you are well.

This attitude will not only uplift others, but make you feel better as well.

Buy a game for a child you know and take time to play with him or her.

Go to a toy store and buy a game that both you and a youngster you know would enjoy. Some games include Monopoly, checkers, Chinese checkers, bingo, Scrabble, or Candyland. Bring the game home and play it with the youngster.

Quality time spent doing something you enjoy and can learn from is invaluable for both of you. The youngster will remember and appreciate your effort long after the game is over. You will also find special pleasure in getting to know the child in a slightly different way.

Make a point of telling others they look good when they do.

Many people take considerable time and pride in their clothing and appearance. It means a great deal to them to look good.

Often we admire these individual's appearance, but neglect to tell the person so. It takes only a moment to let someone know how good he or she looks. Yet these few words can have a great deal of impact, lift someone's spirits, and bolster a person's confidence.

By telling a person he or she looks good, we thank that person for his or her efforts, and we help that person feel better.

Stop and say thank you to a policeman, fireman, postman, or other public official on duty.

When you have some contact with a public servant doing their job, take the time to thank them for the work they are doing. Most public servants go unnoticed. People take for granted the contributions they make. It perks up their day to be noticed, acknowledged, and thanked for their efforts on our behalf.

If someone on the road lets you go ahead of them, or into the lane where that person is driving, take a moment to wave thanks.

We often ask others on the road to let us go ahead of them or squeeze into a lane, and we take it for granted when we are allowed to. We do not register the other driver's consideration or that we are causing that person a moment or two of delay.

When someone is generous to you in this manner, take a moment to wave thanks. The person will feel as if his or her courtesy has been received and that advantage is not being taken.

If someone doesn't give you the full amount of change, do not get angry with them. Ask nicely for the rest of your change, and say you know it must have been an oversight.

It is very easy to make another person feel bad, either directly or by innuendo. This is particularly true if a person does not give you your full change when a purchase is made.

Be careful not to let this happen to you. Assume an oversight on the part of the other. As the Bible instructs, "Always give people the benefit of the doubt." Ask for your change in a manner that will save their feelings. You might say, in a gentle tone, "I'm terribly sorry, there must have been an oversight here," rather than speak harshly or loudly and imply something else.

JULY 15

Be kind and generous to waiters and waitresses in restaurants.

Unfortunately, many people are unpleasant to waiters and waitresses, especially if they are hungry, or if they want to impress someone they are with. Not only is this demeaning to the waiter, but it is demeaning to themselves. If the food comes a little late, or isn't to their liking, the waiter is often the one who bears the brunt of it. People complain greatly of service in restaurants, even when it is up to par.

Be especially pleasant, thankful, and respectful to the waiters and waitresses who are serving you. It is a difficult job, and a kind word from a customer can go a long way for them.

Be generous with your tips as well. A large portion of a waiter's salary is based on tips. Give a little more rather than a little less.

This attitude will also enhance your well-being.

JULY 16

Make a necklace of seashells and give it to a friend as a gift.

Summer is a wonderful time to gather all kinds of seashells at the beach. These can make beautiful ornaments.

Take some time to gather special seashells. Make a tiny hole in each one, and string them on a thread or fine rope. You will make a unique necklace which will provide the beauty of summer to the recipient all year long.

The necklace will also have special meaning because you made it yourself for a friend.

If someone in the family is coming to visit, make sure you call up and include others in the family who might like to see that person too.

Do everything you can to avoid cliques in your family. Don't leave some members out in the cold. Whatever is done to create harmony will ultimately be beneficial to all. When you invite some people from the family over, be sure to call others who might like to see them. Keep family members informed about what's going on. When bonds grow strong, family members can be there for each other during times of need and times of joy.

The very nature of a family is all belonging.

When you've been a guest at someone's home for a day or two, always leave a little gift behind.

It is delightful to receive hospitality and to enjoy someone's home and friendship. If you've been a guest for a day or two (or more) and it is time to leave, make certain you leave the place clean and fresh, and always leave a little token of thanks behind.

This little gift is a way of communicating how thoughtful your host has been to you. Now you are taking a moment to be thoughtful and generous in return.

Visit someone you know who is ill and confined to bed and bring along a book to read to that person.

Many times we do not visit someone who is ill and confined to bed because we do not know what to say. Also, we may be feeling guilty for being well and able to live normally while this person is confined.

Visit someone you know who is confined to home. Before you go, spend a little time finding out the kinds of books and reading material that person is interested in. Whatever it is, bring it and offer to read it to them.

You have no idea how soothing it is for some who are ill to be read to. It may be too strenuous for them to read themselves, or to engage in conversation. Hearing the voice of another reading often feels like an act of love. People feel as though they are being given to unconditionally, without having to give anything back for the time being. Subconsciously, it may also remind them of being read to as a child.

Make some dolls and donate them to the Police Athletic League or the hospital, for sick children to play with.

It is easy and enjoyable to make your own dolls. These dolls can have a distinct personality and bring special joy to children who are needy.

Obtain some cloth, stuffing (cotton or foam), and string. Stuff the cloth, stitch it up (or staple it), use the string to demarcate the parts, and then find something unusual in which to dress the doll. You can find buttons for the eyes, crêpe paper for the hair, and paint a mouth with red lipstick. Let your imagination run wild. Some people have even decorated dolls with leaves and dried flowers.

These dolls will have a special charm. You can then donate them to the Police Athletic League, or bring them to a hospital for sick children to enjoy.

> *The path is not in the sky,*
> *It is in the heart.*
>
> —BUDDHA

Teach a child how to swim.

Children are natural swimmers if they are taught early. The best way for a child to escape fear of the water is to learn how to swim.

Take a child to a pool in your neighborhood, and be gentle and patient in teaching him or her. If you are relaxed and having fun, the child will be relaxed and learn readily. Someday you will also have a friend to go swimming with.

❧

Join in at a party. Reach out, speak up, and make the party fun.

Some of us sit back at parties and wait to be entertained. Unless others speak to us first, we retreat with little to do or say.

A fine way of giving thanks to your host or hostess is to help make the party fun. Find something interesting to talk about. Circulate, tell some jokes, introduce yourself to others, and be interested in what they have to say.

You will have a much better time and help others enjoy themselves too. The host or hostess will be grateful for your input, and very likely you will soon be invited to other parties as well.

❧

If you really loved a movie, buy a couple of extra tickets as you leave, and give them to a friend.

After we see a movie we love, the movie often lingers in our thoughts, and we tell others not to miss it.

This time, as you leave the movie, give a friend a call and ask if they have seen the show. If they haven't, stop at the box office, and buy a couple of extra tickets for them. If there is no one at the box office when you leave, take the time to go back the next day and get the tickets.

If you're at a party, bar, or club and someone approaches you, even if he or she isn't your type, spend some time talking with them. Do not blow them off.

It doesn't take much to be thoughtful and kind to an individual who approaches you, even if he or she is not your type. A few moments spent in pleasant conversation can do a great deal to make the person feel good about themselves and better able to approach someone else later.

If you don't care to continue the association all night, just thank them for talking with you, tell them you enjoyed speaking with them, and mention nicely that there is someone else there you've promised to spend a little time with. This will leave everyone feeling good.

JULY 25

Create a Best Friend Award and give it to your best friend.

Get a large piece of paper and design an attractive wall hanging that reads, Best Friend Award, granted to _____, with the name of your best friend on it. Include anything else you choose: the date, how long you have been friends, and the qualities this person has.

Have the award printed professionally on fine paper, and include an interesting border design. When it is complete, frame it.

Call and invite this friend to dinner. At dinner, present the award. Your friend will be startled and delighted. Think of how proud he or she will be to hang it up for everyone to enjoy.

JULY 26

Write a eulogy of kind remembrance for someone you knew, and send it to the family a few weeks after the person has passed away.

During the first few weeks after the loss of a loved one, there are usually many visitors and calls. Then it grows quieter, and the reality of the loss has more of a chance to sink in. Those left behind then feel more alone.

At this time, a fond remembrance of the person who passed will be deeply appreciated. It lets people know others are still thinking of them and of their loved one, and are in tune with their loss.

Ask to see photos of someone's children or grandchildren.

Everyone loves to show off photos of their children, but many feel embarrassed to do so, as if they are boasting.

Make a special point of asking to see photographs of someone's children or grandchildren. When the photos are shown to you, really look at them and then tell the person how lovely the children are.

This will mean a great deal to your friend. You'll enjoy the experience too.

If you tell someone you're going to call at a certain time of day, make certain you do.

There are few things as disappointing and annoying as waiting for a call that has been promised and does not come. The person waiting and expecting the call may curtail his or her activities until the call comes, or have it on his or her mind all day long.

Not calling when you say you will is also a way of communicating to another that that individual is not so important to you. He or she may just be an afterthought for you after other things have been taken care of. This kind of behavior gives a clear signal you are not someone in whom that person can place his or her trust.

If someone asks you for a reference, take time to give it fully.

We are often asked for references about someone who has worked for us, or asked to be a character reference and write a letter for someone trying to get into a new school or a new job. This is a very important activity, and a wonderful way of giving thanks.

Fulfill this request as soon as you are asked. Don't delay and keep everyone waiting. Find the good points of the person and communicate them fully. If there is any realistic problem with the person, put it in the best possible light.

A person's good name is one of their most valuable possessions. Do not hesitate to speak out for someone who needs your support.

Take a child to the pet store, buy him or her a fish tank, and fill it with interesting fish, coral, rocks, and plants.

Fish tanks are wonderful, educational experiences for children. While buying one and filling it with fish, rocks, corals, and plants, the youngster learns a great deal about sea life. Once the fish tank is home and he or she maintains it, the child also learns how to care for other life forms and about responsibility. It is soothing and enjoyable to have the many colored fish swimming around.

A gift like this offers the possibility of ongoing adventure, education, enjoyment, and growth. It is a fine experience to initiate for a youngster and spend time sharing.

When you're with someone who is unhappy, find two ways to make them smile.

When you are with someone today who is unhappy, find two ways to make them smile. Purposely change the atmosphere and unleash the child within both of you.

You might suddenly do something silly, sing a song, tell a joke, make a face, or otherwise change their focus. Invite the person to go to the park with you and sit on the swings.

This does not mean that the problem is unimportant and does not need to be attended to, but often the best way to get a new point of view about something is to have a good laugh at yourself.

When someone tells you about a project they are undertaking, refrain from saying anything negative.

It is easy to find reasons why we cannot or should not try something new. When someone comes to us with a new idea, we usually try to find problems with it, and, even if we do not mean to, we dampen the person's enthusiasm.

The most important aspect of the project is simply that the person is willing to try something new. When you are asked about it, find reasons why the project will succeed. Acknowledge the person for his or her courage.

The person will feel you are on his or her team and be grateful for your vote of confidence. As time passes, the person will see any problems with the project, and know what to do. Whether or not the person chooses to continue, he or she will predominantly remember that you believed in the project.

Keep your fears to yourself but share your courage.
—ROBERT LOUIS STEVENSON

When you speak to others, call them by their name. If someone has a unique or lovely name, tell that person so.

The sweetest sound to others is the sound of their own name. If you remember a person's name and use it, that will let others know you are attentive to that individual and that he or she is not just one of the mass of people who wander in and out of your life.

The person whose name you use will be affected by it and respond more warmly to you. You will make that person feel unique and special. If you go the extra step and mention that his or her name is lovely, that will only add to mutual good feelings.

If someone speaks ill of another, find some good things to say about that person.

Often we hear someone speaking negatively about someone we know. Rather than join in the gossip, or ask for more details, why not turn the whole conversation around. Find some good things to say about the person. You will give a balanced picture and protect this person's reputation, and you may stop unkind comments from being made.

Some people live on hearing bad things about others. Not only is this destructive behavior for the person listening and telling, it can only have a hurtful effect upon those they are speaking of as well.

AUGUST 4

Choose a person who is close to you and do something for your friend for no reason at all.

It is easy to go out and buy presents. It is more personal and interesting to actually give of ourselves by doing something for the person that you know he or she may need to have done. Some examples are finding a blind date, helping to plant a garden, walking the dog for a week, raking the lawn, picking up clothes from the dry cleaner, dropping off a rented videotape. There are endless possibilities. Be creative.

This gift will create a personal link between you and will remain with both of you long after it is done.

AUGUST 5

When you find a large insect trapped in your house, rather than killing it, help it find its way out.

Although it might be easy to kill an insect that is bothering us, it takes only a few more minutes to help it find its way outside. We share our lives and earth with creatures of all kinds. Although an insect may seem insignificant to us, it has a life too, and we have been blessed with the ability to protect it.

This sensitivity and caring for all life forms will make our time here richer and more meaningful.

AUGUST 6

Find memorabilia left by someone from an older generation in your family and share it with someone young.

It is extremely enriching to keep the connection between generations in a family alive. Do you have something meaningful left behind by your parent, grandparent, or great grandparent that you could share with your child or grandchild?

Some examples could be photos, letters, books the person loved, stories he or she told, an old jacket, a scarf or a hat, a watch, a wedding ring, deeds of worth the person performed, or just your own memories about what was contributed to you.

AUGUST 7

When you tell someone you are going to do something for them, or give something to them, do it right away.

We often take our time fulfilling a commitment we said we would give or do, such as raking the leaves in the garden, taking someone out to dinner, lending a book, or purchasing tickets to a game. This leaves the person waiting, not knowing for sure whether or when the commitment will materialize. If too much time passes, the person may even feel uncomfortable receiving it at all.

When you make an offer of a service or goods, deliver right away. This is a way of truly giving to another, without causing that person to pay the price of anxiety about whether it will happen. It tells the person that you are giving with a full heart.

When you're invited to a baby shower, make something for the new baby with your own hands.

Preparing for the arrival of a new baby is a delightful, long range project. There are endless ways to welcome a new baby which can be especially meaningful to the new parents and you.

If you are invited to a baby shower, or know a family who is expecting, make something unique and individual with your own hands. You could knit or sew a blanket or sweater, create a wall hanging, embroider a cap, or perhaps frame some family pictures to be put in the new baby's room or crib. You could make decorations for the crib or even draw your own little book for the baby when he or she is old enough to look at it.

Taking the time to make something with your own hands becomes a special contribution of love.

When you're listening, really listen. Don't rehearse what you're going to say next.

So many times we can't even begin to hear another person because we're paying so much attention to the voices inside our head. Many people are far more concerned with how they will respond and the impression they're making than about what the other person is saying.

Give your full attention to the other person. Forget about yourself for a while. Really listen when you're listening. Respond spontaneously. Being there fully for another is a gift of love.

Be a good receiver. Accept graciously.

For some it is easy to give all day long, but difficult to receive. It is as important to accept from others as it is to give. When you allow others to give to you, you help them feel good about themselves. You let them know they have something worth giving and are able to make you happy.

When we simply give all the time without receiving, it can be a way of creating obligation and guilt. True giving always includes receiving. When we give freely, without necessarily wanting something back, the universe always returns our gift. At that time, it is necessary for us to be able to receive graciously. This is a beautiful way of saying thank you.

If someone owes you something, see if you can let the debt go.

If someone owes you something—money, a phone call, love—whatever it is, see if you can let the debt pass. Let the person be free. Hold nothing against them.

You will not only free the other, you will free and enrich yourself as well.

Take good care of your friendships by checking in with friends regularly.

Make sure you keep in touch with your friends. Remember their birthdays and anniversaries. Send them little notes. If they are not feeling well, check in and see how they are doing. Offer to stop in at the market for them. If a friend is facing some particular challenge, do not hesitate to offer your help before being asked for it.

Like a wise gardener, we must till the soil of relationships frequently and pull out the weeds so that flowers of good feelings can bloom.

> *To care for things makes the whole world come to life.*
>
> —ZEN SAYING

Set up a fund for charity in someone's name.

It is a relatively simple matter to set up a fund for charity in someone's name. (That person can be dead or alive. It should be someone who cares about or has worked particularly with that charity.) Sometimes people wish to send a gift for that person. Simply ask that this gift be money dedicated to that fund. Even small amounts add up.

Establish an account at your bank and designate it to the charity of choice. Then make a public announcement. Doing so will give others an opportunity to give both to the person and to the charity at the same time.

Have a ball game with someone who doesn't usually play.

Rustle up a game of stick ball or handball with someone who usually doesn't play—your wife, neighbor, cousin, child. This game will be new and fun. It will break the person out of his or her usual mold and open up new doors of enjoyment for the two of you.

Whenever we help someone else be playful, it makes us more playful as well.

Invite three or four people to dinner at the beach.

Summer lasts a short time. It is easy to let the beautiful days go by. Call up three or four people you know are available and invite them to an informal, surprise picnic dinner at the beach tonight.

Buy or make a bunch of sandwiches and a jug of iced tea or lemonade. Pack a volleyball and a blanket and make the end of the day a delightful time.

Even though it is only a few hours and all the preparations are simple, you will all go home refreshed and delighted.

List a few people who you respect very much, dwell on their achievements, and emulate them.

There is little as valuable in this world as self-respect. Respect for ourselves and our actions is in itself a way of giving thanks.

It is worthwhile to think about the people you respect. Dwell on their achievements. What qualities and values do they possess that have gained your respect? Some examples could be persistence, loyalty, the willingness to live by principles, or being there for others.

Look over the list carefully. This list represents your core values in life, whether or not you are presently living up to it.

Today, choose one item from the list and emulate it. You'll be amazed at the changes this will bring in your life and in how you feel about yourself. (You might take other items later on, or add to the list as the days go on.)

If something displeases you, just let it go.

If something displeases you, like a comment your mother-in-law made, a disappointment in a relationship, a rejection on a project, or bad weather on an important day, rather than dwell upon it, just let it go. Walk away and put it to the side. Engage in a new activity and turn your attention to something else.

Not only will your displeasure vanish and your mood improve, but whatever it was that displeased you will look different later on. And, most importantly, you will have not spoiled your day or the day of others.

AUGUST 18

Go to an event—a wedding, communion, graduation, or a funeral that you ordinarily might not attend.

It means a great deal to others when we attend special occasions in their lives. Sometimes it is difficult or inconvenient to do so. Our first response might be to refuse, and just send a gift or a note. However, the support you give at weddings, anniversaries, baptisms, funerals, and other occasions resonates way beyond the event itself. Make an extra effort to be there. It will mean a great deal.

AUGUST 19

Plant a tree today.

Trees can be planted all over the country, or even abroad. There are agencies that will do this for you, or you might wish to do it yourself.

It is inspiring to plant a small sapling and watch it grow. Along with nurturing the environment, as we watch the tree grow and become strong, we see that life constantly renews itself. For children, the joy of watching a tree grow will stay with them for the rest of their lives.

Or, if someone you love has passed away or someone you know has sustained a loss, why not plant a tree in memory of that person? Each loss can bring new gain.

Open a savings account for a poor child, and deposit just a little bit each week. See how the money grows. Every few months give it to him or her.

If you put just a little bit each week into a savings account for a poor child, it can make a huge difference to that youngster. Find a child you know who is needy and open an account for the youngster. You can take the money out every few months and present whatever has accumulated to him or her. Think about how he or she will look forward to it, and how good you will both feel.

Establish a charity box in your home or office for stray coins and spare change.

We often find stray pennies, nickels, even dimes and quarters both in our homes and out on the street. Instead of leaving them there lying around, make the effort to pick them up and collect them in your pocket. Put them in a box you establish for a charity such as the American Cancer Society, Muscular Dystrophy Foundation, or Gay Men's Health Crisis or the next time you see a box for charity on the counter of a luncheonette, dry cleaner, or other location, drop in the stray coins.

These coins add up. The few moments you spent collecting them will help those in need.

Ask yourself what treat you would really like today. Give it to yourself. Ask someone you're close to what treat he or she would like. See if you can give it that person.

Most of us assume that treats are for special occasions or times when we have done something to deserve them. We walk around feeling deprived, wishing others would think of us, or extend some warmth.

However, we can be like another person to ourselves. If we stop regularly and ask ourselves what we would really like as a treat, and then give it to ourselves, our days would be much brighter, and we would feel well cared for. The same is true for those people we are close to. Ask them what they would like if they could have it. Once they tell you, see if you can get it for them.

Be creative. Some treats could be a long walk in the park, going to a movie, an outrageous lipstick, reading a new book, a massage, or quality time with a friend. Tune in, ask yourself and another, and then give it open handedly.

No matter what mood you are in, bring a spirit of good cheer with you wherever you go.

It is easy to let ourselves become depressed if things aren't going as we wish they would. We then go out into our day, exuding gloom and irritation wherever we go. Needless to say, this just compounds difficulties, not only for ourselves but for everyone we meet.

No matter how you feel inside today, decide to cheer up everyone else. Be a messenger of happy tidings. Dress in a way that will uplift others—wear lovely colors or a special cologne. Smile and offer words of encouragement.

As you do this all day long, see what happens to your own feelings of gloom. Most of us allow our actions to be run by our feelings. Why not let your feelings be generated by the positive actions you choose?

Be happy. It is a way of being wise.
—COLETTE

Take a step to break an addiction you have, be it to alcohol, drugs, gambling, unhealthy food, or anything else.

Addictions can rule our lives, making us feel that it is impossible to let them go. However, we are inherently stronger than we think and once a firm decision is made to break an addiction all kinds of help will appear.

An addiction can be a strong habit that helps us escape from personal problems. One way to weaken that negative habit is to replace it with another habit that is equally strong, counteracts the negative habit, and is healthy and enjoyable. Another important ingredient is to get help facing the underlying problems and start building a life that is workable.

There are organizations such as Alcoholics Anonymous, Gambling Anonymous, Overeaters Anonymous, and Synanon that have fine programs to help. There are also many kinds of alternative treatments.

Choose to believe only positive thoughts today.

All day long we are bombarded with various thoughts, messages, and expectations. It is easy to go down a dark alley, believe the worst, and create unnecessary stress and anxiety for ourselves and others. Although we may not have the power to control what is happening, we can always choose how we will respond. We can choose our thoughts and beliefs.

Today consciously and purposefully decide to believe only positive thoughts—thoughts that inspire and uplift you. No matter how difficult something may seem, find a positive aspect to it. Choose to ignore prophets of doom.

If you do this all day long, you will be truly astonished at the powerful effect it has on your life. Not only will you have more energy, fun, and productivity, but you will spark this in others as well.

Mail a tiny gift in an envelope to someone close to you.

It's easy enough to put some small seashells, potpourri, gum, stickers, ribbons, or other simple present in an envelope and mail it to a friend. You can add a small note that says, "Hope you enjoy this!" The mere fact that you are thinking of your friend will mean more than the treat itself.

Help end world hunger.

Across the world, there are many nations and children who suffer from devastating hunger and droughts. Fortunately, organizations exist, such as the Hunger Project, World Crisis Network and UNICEF, which are dedicated to wiping out world hunger. These organizations need your help, both personally and financially. (Even just telling others about them and the problems they are tackling makes a difference.)

Countless deaths from starvation can and are being prevented. Share the bounty you have in your life by helping in any way you can.

Find two good traits in someone who you don't like.

Find some seashells or pieces of driftwood and send them to friends as gifts.

It's very easy to be critical and find something wrong with everyone we meet. This can simply be a distorted way of making ourselves look good. However, when we live this way we take away our own joy. We find ourselves living in a world of enemies instead of friends.

Find two good traits in someone who you don't like. Dwell on them when you see the person. See how beautifully they respond, and how your own feelings about the person changes. The more people you are willing to feel good about, the better you will feel about yourself as well.

It is wonderful to spend time collecting a wide variety seashells on the beach. You will find joy in giving them as gifts to others.

You can string the seashells together for a necklace, paste them on a canvas as a collage, or paint something on each one and then give them out as gifts to friends. Or, at the beach, you might also find beautiful driftwood, sea glass, rocks, or a variety of matter washed up from the ocean.

Your friends will be charmed by this personal, thoughtful touch.

Find a wrong you committed and repair it today.

Even though it may seem painful to admit we've done wrong, or offended somebody, we can get great pleasure from setting it right. It is much easier to correct errors than we imagine.

We can start by apologizing. Whether or not the apology is accepted, just the fact that we've offered it begins to set things right. The next step is to take the opposite action, either with that person or with somebody else. If the person you've wronged is willing to discuss it with you, you can ask what they'd like you to do to make it up. If they're not willing to participate, just take this new, positive action with someone else.

Instead of actually correcting and reversing errors, most people hold onto guilt. Guilt is simply a negative replacement for taking the positive action of repair. Guilt is not productive. New action is. Once new, positive actions are taken, guilt flies out the window for good.

Make a list of quotes and sayings that inspire you. Write them on lovely paper, and once a week, send one to a friend.

Quotations and meaningful sayings have much more impact when you share them with a friend. Make a list of the quotes and sayings that have been important to you. Buy some beautiful stationery, and write one on each page. Then, once a week, take a page and mail it to a friend.

You will be sending little angels out into the universe.

ROSH HASHANA

Learn about the Jewish New Year. Take time to review your deeds.

The Jewish New Year is a time of prayer, recollection, charity, repentance, and rejoicing, which falls during the months of September or October. Families gather to pray together and join in communal meals. Apples are dipped in honey to symbolize the wish for a sweet and fruitful new year.

Preparation for the New Year requires an individual to ask for and grant forgiveness. He or she must say to all those they know, "If I have offended you in any manner, please forgive me." Each person is also required to grant forgiveness as well.

YOM KIPPUR

Spend the day more quietly than usual. Think deeply about the ways you may have harmed another. Ask for forgiveness both from the person and from God.

Yom Kippur, which is always seven days after Rosh Hashana, is the holiest day of the year for the Jewish people. The end of the last prayers of the night marks the final time of judgment. The books are then closed and the individual's destiny for the future year is sealed—who will live, who will die. It is said that prayer, charity, and repentance will cancel the stern decree.

The day is spent in continual prayer, fasting, and deep repentance. Prayers for forgiveness are offered to God, and the resolve to make teshuvah is strengthened. Teshuvah is the process of returning to the will of God.

If someone criticizes you, think about what they are saying before you rush to defend yourself.

The minute someone criticizes us about anything we usually flare into anger or immediately start to defend ourselves. At the very least, we see the person as an opponent. Friendly feelings quickly fade away.

If you receive criticism, stop a moment and consider what the person is saying to you. Is he or she saying it to help? Is there some truth in the points being made? Are there ways in which you might correct your behavior that would be better for all?

No matter what you are feeling at the moment, thank the person for their observations, and tell him or her that you will think about what was said. If there is something to correct, why not do it now?

The ways you think you are,
Not the ways you really are,
Are the bars on your own personal prison.

—ANONYMOUS

Buy a bottle of wine or champagne for someone you care about, and put it in their refrigerator.

Buy a fine bottle of wine or champagne and quietly place it in your friend's refrigerator. They will find your gift when you are not there. How thrilled that person will be. If the person does not drink alcoholic beverages, purchase a bottle of sparkling cider or other delicious fruit drink.

Be aware of the contributions made by the labor force of our nation.

Typically Labor Day (always the Monday following the first full weekend in September) marks the end of summer and that it's time to go back to the school and work year. It was instituted in order to recognize the contributions made by the labor force of our nation.

While you are celebrating at your barbecue or other gathering, mention of our indebtedness to those who have built this nation through their labor. Explore what issues the labor unions are dealing with now and how we can best support the workers of our land.

When you see a woman on the street with a child, stop a moment and tell her how beautiful her child is.

Child rearing is an extremely consuming, demanding, and sometimes strenuous occupation. Mothers get little daily acknowledgment for the work they put in.

When you see a woman with a child, stop for a moment and tell her how beautiful her child is. In effect, you will be telling her what a fine job she is doing. She will feel grateful and proud.

SEPTEMBER 4

Ask to see pictures of someone's summer vacation.

Everyone loves to review the pictures and memories of their summer vacation with friends. In this way fond memories are relived, which becomes twice as enjoyable.

Take the time specifically to ask your friends to show you photographs or videos of their summer vacation. Give these your full attention and allow yourself to enjoy the memories with them.

SEPTEMBER 5

Reach out to the children in developing nations.

The needs of children in the developing nations are so great, that even small efforts and amounts of money on our part make an enormous difference. For example, the Micro Nutrient Deficiency Program at UNICEF (United Nations International Children's Emergency Fund) corrects nutritional deficiencies which can make the difference between health and severe medical problems for a child. For a small sum a child can have enough vitamin A to prevent blindness and improve all health and iodine deficiency, which is the leading cause of mental retardation, can be eliminated.

While these sums are a pittance to us, the children that they go to need the money desperately. Call or write to UNICEF and see how you can contribute.

SEPTEMBER 6

Stop in at the local senior citizens' center. Spend an hour with the elderly.

Too many people toss seniors aside as if their lives are over. Actually, the opposite is true. In many places of the world (and in most ancient traditions), the elderly are the most revered people in their society. According to the Bible, old age was something that Abraham *requested* happen to man, so that he may be distinguished and honored for his years.

Older people are a powerful resource for wisdom, healing, and just plain fun. Many have a wealth of stories and life experiences that could be touching and helpful for you.

Call your Chamber of Commerce or a local chapter of American Association of Retired Persons, and find out where your senior citizen centers are. Learn about their hours, schedule of activities, and special projects. Advise them that you would like to spend some time with the elderly. There may even be ways you could be specifically useful with some of these projects.

SEPTEMBER 7

On the road, when you see children looking at you through their car windows, wave hello.

Today, children are taught to be careful in so many ways that they may come to feel that the world is an entirely dangerous place. To counteract this, when you see children on the road looking at you through their car windows, wave hello. Give them a smile. Make a funny face. A moment of playfulness together will help them feel cheerful and realize there is also warmth and friendliness around.

Be a grandparent to your grandparents. Take them out to lunch and spoil them. Tell them what they mean to you and how proud you are of them.

All year long, grandparents shower grandchildren with special attention, admiration, gifts, and love. On Grandparent's Day (the second Sunday in September) turn this around. Be a grandparent to your grandparents. Really spoil and fuss over them.

Take them to their favorite place for a delicious lunch. Bring along cards or flowers to present once you get there. Find the qualities about them you truly admire and tell them how proud you are of them.

A day like this will live in their hearts for a very long time.

If you are having a party and lots of your friends are coming, invite neighbors whom you do not know.

When you are having a large party at your home, your neighbors will become aware of it. Many cars will park near your house, or if you live in an apartment house, the sounds of people enjoying themselves will penetrate the walls.

When a large party is happening nearby, it is easy to feel lonely or left out. If at all possible, extend an invitation to those who live near you and who will be aware of the festivities. Whether they choose to attend, this will make them feel welcome and cared for.

SEPTEMBER 9

Build a model airplane with a child.

Children love to work on projects, especially with an adult who cares. Choose and build a model airplane with a youngster. As well as being educationally rewarding, this quality time you spend together will show the child you care.

Great is the human who has not lost his childlike heart.

—MENCIUS

SEPTEMBER 10

Make sure you always signal for right and left turns in your car, rather than turning suddenly.

Sensitivity and awareness on the highway goes a long way toward creating a harmonious society. Be conscious of others when you're driving. Don't turn suddenly and cause others to stop short. Make sure you signal for right and left turns in your car well before turning.

The extra courtesy and time you take in doing this could prevent harm to yourself or someone else.

Volunteer at your church, synagogue, or place of worship or reflection.

There are endless ways in which your time and energy can make a difference at your place of worship or reflection. Many programs are offered that require helping hands, including collecting food and clothing for those less fortunate. Some religious places have active programs for visiting the sick.

Call and ask how you can make a difference. Perhaps you have something specific you'd like to offer—a class to teach or some other kind of contribution. Be creative. There are many people who would greatly benefit from your knowledge, time, skills, and life experience. You'll be surprised to discover how much you have to give.

If someone is repeating himself or herself, don't stop that person. Let him or her finish. Listen as though it were the first time you heard the story.

Most people have a fear of repeating themselves, and yet we all do it unconsciously. Next time you notice someone doing it, listen as though it were the first time you heard the story. This will protect the person from feeling embarrassed. It might also allow you to hear things in the story you didn't hear before.

The Bible instructs not to make people feel embarrassed by publicly telling them that they are repeating themselves. To help another save face publicly is one of the most important deeds you can do.

If you see someone about to get into trouble, make sure you warn him or her about it.

Sometimes we see something coming that can or will cause another harm. This could be a business venture, relationship, or activity that they are about to embark on.

At times like these, do not remain silent. Even though the person might not like your warning, or even take it, in the long run you will feel better knowing that you did all you could to forestall the problem. And when the person does listen, how wonderful it will be to know that you were able to help another by caring enough to speak up and extend a warning.

At a service place (beauty parlor, car wash, etc.), tell the service people what a nice job they're doing.

When you're at a beauty parlor, garage, car wash, manicurist, shoemaker, any kind of service place, make a point of really looking at the work the people are doing, and compliment them on the task they are performing. The service person will be gratified to see that his or her work is noticed, lifting his or her spirits. It is also meaningful for you to truly notice the work of others and the efforts they are making.

Notice when you are either overwhelming another or being too withdrawn, and adjust your behavior.

When we are with others we often fail to notice how our behavior affects them. We might be excited and speaking very quickly but, instead of generating enthusiasm, we might be overwhelming them. On the other hand, we might tend to be overly quiet and withdrawn, causing others to feel uncomfortable.

Notice how your behavior affects those you are with and adjust it so that you create a feeling of harmony. If you are overwhelming the other person, calm down a bit. If your reticence is causing discomfort, find something to say.

This effort on your part will not only be appreciated, it will bear wonderful fruit in your relationships.

Tell others there is a higher purpose in life.

To know there is a higher purpose to our lives that brings meaning, peace, and reconciliation to many events that happen that we cannot immediately accept. We may not know exactly what our higher purpose is, but just to know it exists and to dwell on that fact is the beginning of further discoveries.

When someone else is in the throes of difficulty, comfort that person with this knowledge. Doing so will bring harmony to events and individuals that may seem to be in disarray.

The greatest use of life is to spend it on something that will outlast it.
—WILLIAM JAMES

If a child or friend is scared or worried about something, even if you don't understand why, listen quietly to how that child or friend feels.

Children, and also adults, have many secret worries and fears. Sometimes they might seem foolish or irrational and we try to laugh them off.

If a child or friend is scared or worried about something, even if you don't understand why, listen quietly to how he or she feels. Don't tell the child or your friend that he or she is silly or that there is nothing to worry about. That only makes the person feel more alone with his or her fears. Listen to all the details related to this fear.

Even though you may not have a solution, listening, without criticism or advice, is helpful. Many will feel that they are loved. Often they will go on to find solutions for themselves.

Fly a kite with a child.

Kites are fun. There are all kinds of kites to fly, even those you can paint yourself. Buy or make a few kites, take a child or a friend to a field, park, or the beach, and enjoy flying the kites.

You'll discover all kinds of things about the wind, the sky, the day, and each other. Most of all you will have a wonderful time.

Enroll in a class or attend a lecture about something you've always wanted to learn.

We all have secret interests that we plan to learn more about one day. Sometimes these interests are buried so deep that we forget completely about them.

Enroll in a class, or even one lecture, about something you've always wanted to learn. You'll be amazed at how good you will feel, as if new doors are opening for you.

Volunteer your time at the library to read stories to young children.

Many libraries have special rooms for children's books. Children love to be read to and to be told stories. Some libraries have reading hours when librarians read to children, but in many libraries this activity is not available (or if it is available, it is only on a limited basis).

Volunteer a little time every week and offer a live reading hour for young children. The librarian will help you choose books that are appropriate. The little ones will love it, and so will you.

Teach someone a healthy habit, like the importance of drinking lots of fresh water all day long—walking—or eating at least one fresh vegetable a day.

When you go to the doctor, dentist, optometrist, or any medical practitioner, leave a box of cookies after your visit as a thank you. Ask that they not only be shared with the staff, but with the other patients as well.

We assume that most people have healthy habits, or at least know what habits are conducive to good health. But this is not true. There is so much information about healthy food and exercise practices that many people feel overwhelmed and simply block it all out. They are not aware that just one or two healthy habits practiced daily can contribute significantly to their well-being.

Teach someone one healthy habit, like the importance of drinking lots of fresh water each day, or walking regularly, or eating just one fresh vegetable a day.

If the person does not feel overwhelmed with instructions and takes on something he or she can truly do, you will have made a difference in his or her lifestyle. Pretty soon that person will feel so good one or two more habits will be taken on.

We often think that paying a bill is sufficient thanks for a doctor, dentist, optometrist, or any person who serves us well. How nice it would be to bring a concrete, specific token of thanks, like a box of cookies. These cookies can be enjoyed not only by the service person, but by the staff and other patients.

SEPTEMBER 23

If you find yourself swearing, stop it.

Some people swear automatically and unconsciously as a way of letting off steam. They do not realize that through this process they are creating a negative atmosphere. Words are powerful and impact both the environment and those listening. Negative, destructive words offend and disturb others.

When you catch yourself swearing, stop it. Find another way to deal with your disappointment or stress. Take deep breaths, go on a fast walk, stop and count to twenty. Carefully change the swear words you use to neutral ones. See how much better you'll feel in the long run.

He who has control over his tongue is greater than a hero in battle.
—SWAMI SHIVANANDA

SEPTEMBER 24

Return loans promptly.

Once someone loans us something, it's easy to feel as if it's our own. Sometimes we forget this loan is still the property of another and that in fact they may still have a need for it. (This is also true for financial loans.)

Be as prompt as possible about returning things—books, umbrellas, sleds—others have loaned you. This is a fine way of thanking them for their thoughtfulness and not taking advantage of their good will.

Do not listen to someone telling a secret you should not hear. Don't tell another's secret either.

It is so tempting to listen to a secret someone is telling that is not for your ears. By listening, you are betraying another's faith. Gently tell the person who is revealing the secret that it is better to respect the other person's privacy and that you would not like to have a secret of yours, which was told in confidence, repeated to others.

Also, if someone asks you to keep a secret, be very careful to do so.

Let someone with a few items go ahead of you in line at the supermarket.

Nobody likes standing on line. Most of us are in a great rush and eager to get to what we are doing next. But waiting in line can be a wonderful opportunity not only to show consideration to others, but to learn patience.

While waiting on line be aware of your surroundings. Who else is in line with you? Is there someone behind you with just a few items? If so, why not be generous and let them go ahead of you? It will only cost you a few extra moments.

When we stop rushing and pushing and just exist in the moment our lives take on a new flavor.

If something bothers you in your friendship, communicate it to your friend simply and honestly. Don't let resentment build.

The biggest gift you can give another is honest communication. This does not mean dumping on the other person, but carefully explaining how you are feeling and not allowing resentment to build.

Responsible communication is a wonderful way of thanking a person and telling them how much he or she means to you. To communicate responsibly, do not blame the other person for your feelings or what you think has gone wrong. Simply say, "This is how I am feeling right now. This is what I want and need." Take responsibility for what is going on inside of you. Make clear statements and requests.

Resentment is poison. It corrodes everything it touches. No relationship can thrive when resentment is allowed to build.

Open or hold the door for someone.

It is easy to rush through life oblivious to those who are around us and even inadvertently slam doors in people's faces. It only takes an extra moment to hold open a door for someone in a building, a room, a car, or an elevator. This extra courtesy and thoughtfulness brings a moment of kind concern, makes the other feel cared for, and gives you an opportunity to say thank you to life.

If you find yourself wanting to tell a lie to someone, stop midstream and correct it.

Lies come in a variety of forms—not just outright lies. Exaggerations, insinuations, and embellishments are also lies. Lying includes all kinds of statements to others that bend the truth.

Though some of this may seem harmless, in the long run it is not. Lying causes confusion, can prompt others to take actions that are not in their best interest, and stirs up hopes and expectations that may never be fulfilled.

As soon as you find yourself telling a lie, correct your statement. Try hard to find and to speak the actual truth.

Not only will this exercise strengthen you and clarify your thinking and actions, it will be inspiring and helpful for those you speak to as well.

Before you go to sleep tonight, think of two people who are close to you and consciously think well of them.

Our thoughts for others are powerful. If we take time to send good wishes and positive thoughts to another, the person can feel uplifted. It is uplifting for you as well to fill your mind with loving, positive thoughts just as you go to sleep.

Go pumpkin picking with a friend or child.

Pumpkin patches are beautiful in autumn. It is lovely to spend time on a beautiful afternoon picking pumpkins and bringing them home.

You can use these pumpkins in a variety of ways. Put a few outside to decorate your home. Use some to make delicious pumpkin pies. Take the seeds out of pumpkins to bake and eat. (Pumpkin seeds are delicious and healthy for you.) Last but not least, reserve a few pumpkins to cut out faces for Halloween time.

Join in a fund-raising effort such as a telethon, a walk for cancer, or a walk for AIDS.

There are many fund-raising efforts in which you can take an active part. There are walks to raise money for cancer, AIDS, Multiple Sclerosis. There are telethons, as well as fund-raising parties and dances.

Pick a fund-raising effort that is meaningful to you and become involved. Your participation will reap benefits for yourself and others.

Don't interrupt when someone is speaking to you.

Most people only listen to others with about one third of their attention. Many are busy thinking of what they will say in response, and after hearing only a portion of what the other is saying, quickly interrupt.

Make a point of not interrupting when someone is speaking to you. Even if you have something burning to say, or realize what the other person is going to say, give that person the courtesy of finishing up.

Being interrupted is jarring for many. It also says clearly that what they have to say doesn't mean so much and that your response is more important to you.

Make a list of three things you could do to improve your current relationship with a friend or loved one. Do at least one or two.

It is easy to dwell on what's wrong with a relationship or how we want the other person to change. When we realize we can't change the other person, we often feel like a failure.

Turn this pattern around. Forget the other for a moment. Make a list of three things *you* could do to improve your current relationship. Do at least one or two. See the difference it makes in you. You'll feel more in control of things and better about yourself.

If you keep taking these positive actions to improve the relationship, it will become clear what your next step should be.

Love is never lost. If not reciprocated, it will
flow back and soften and purify the heart.
—Washington Irving

Be on time to appointments.

It is an act of gracious respect to be somewhere when you say you will, and not leave others waiting. There are many forms of theft: One of them is stealing someone's time. Being on time shows consideration for another's schedule and feelings. It causes others to see you as someone who can be counted on. In this manner, the entire appointment will get off to a good start. If you have a hard time being on time, aim to be there five minutes early. Your thoughtfulness will pay off in many ways.

Bring someone apple picking. Take the harvest home and make a fresh apple pie.

The earth gives to us bountifully. When we joyously receive what is given it is a way of giving thanks. Take someone with you picking apples and see for yourself the abundant goodness of life. It's fun to be together outdoors.

Bring the harvest back home and bake a fresh pie or two. Share the pies with your family or neighbors. All will benefit from your lovely day.

Rake the leaves on your neighbor's lawn.

Autumn leaves are beautiful and abundant. One day when you are raking your own, go next door and rake your neighbor's lawn as well. They will be delighted at your thoughtfulness. It's a small but lovely way of saying, "I'm glad you're next door."

Buy your pet a bone, catnip, a special ball, or other treat he or she loves.

Our pets are touched when we bring home little treats. This is a fine way of thanking them for their unqualified affection and love.

Take time today to buy something special that your pet loves. It could be a bone, catnip, special ball, toy, or other treat. When you give it to him or her, take a little while to stay and play. This will enhance both the gift and your pet's feeling of being appreciated.

Find three ways in which a person is unique and tell him or her.

Many people are not aware of their personal uniqueness. They feel like one of a crowd, not special in any way. Although there may be security in blending into the group, everybody needs to know and feel that there is something unique and special about them. And there always is.

Find three ways a person you are close to is special, and then tell that person about it. This will enhance his or her self-image, give each person a new way of thinking about his or her life, and present the possibility of developing unusual qualities.

We are constantly invited to be what we are.
—HENRY DAVID THOREAU

Create a special photo album for your child and fill it with pictures of him or her at all stages of life.

There is nothing more delightful than to look back at ourselves at all different stages of our lives. Often photos of certain years get lost, and we are left with blank spots in our memories.

Buy a photograph album and put in photos of your child from the time he or she was born until the present. Keep this album going as your youngster grows up. You can also include memorabilia of special events, such as programs from your child's graduations, certificates or awards he or she wins, or special birthday invitations.

This collection will become a real treasure that he or she will be most grateful and delighted to receive from you when your youngster is fully grown. At that time, you can start another one, noting the new stages of your young person's life.

OCTOBER 11

Start your child (or yourself) learning a foreign language.

There are many benefits of learning a foreign language. We learn to see and hear the world from another's point of view. We can read foreign books in the original version, and are able to converse with an entire group of new people. When we travel, it is much easier to know and be known by others. Needless to say, this opens many new doors and makes our lives much richer.

It is fairly simple to begin learning a foreign language. There are many classes offered in schools, continuing education programs, and on audiotape. Have your children choose a language they might be interested in and get them started.

OCTOBER 12
Columbus Day

Learn about the American Indians, the original inhabitants of our land, and share that knowledge with someone.

This is the day Columbus discovered America. When he arrived, the Native Americans had a bountiful culture of their own. Learn about the fascinating Native American history, customs, handiwork, and beliefs.

There are many books available on the subject in the library, as well as exhibits in museums, and art galleries and stores that feature art, handiwork, and jewelry made by Native Americans today. The Heard Museum in Phoenix, Arizona, an internationally acclaimed museum, is devoted to exhibits that promote appreciation and respect for the Native Americans. You can contact them for information about other museums, galleries, and stores in your area.

When you are reading a newspaper or magazine today and notice an article that would be relevant or meaningful to someone you know, cut it out and send it to them.

Many of our friends and acquaintances have varied interests. We often read articles that would be especially interesting to them, and just let it pass by.

Take a few extra minutes to cut out the article, put it in an envelope with a little note, and send it to the person who would be interested.

Sending someone an article shows that person that he or she is on your mind. They will be touched by your thoughtfulness, and the article will have extra meaning as well.

Go to a homeless shelter and provide a few personal items to the people there.

There are many items we have that we no longer use: clothing, books, audiotapes, plants, artwork, old watches or other pieces of jewelry. Go through your possessions and take some things that you no longer use to a homeless shelter. When you give these items to others who will use and cherish them, they will also realize that they are not completely forgotten.

Buy newspapers or any other items produced by the homeless. Help them stand on their feet again.

If you see a blind person, ask if you can help them.

If you see a blind person alone, it only takes a moment to help them on their way. Some people feel that they may be intruding, but if you gently ask the blind person if he or she would like some assistance, you may hear the answer yes. Even if the blind person does not want the assistance, he or she will be touched that someone has asked.

You don't have to accompany the sightless person far—even just a few blocks along his or her way.

Give a tape (or CD) that you love to someone else whom you feel might love it.

If there is a tape of music, affirmations, instruction, or inspiration you listen to and really love, why not buy another one and give it to a friend?

We make a living by what we get,
but we make a life by what we give.
—NORMAN MCEVAN

Be a resource for someone who needs help or information.

Sometimes others are working on projects and need information that we have or can get. They may not have the time to obtain it for themselves, or don't know how to go about gathering it.

Offer yourself as a resource for such an individual. Spend a little time collecting the information or contacts you have and be generous about sharing them. (Or, if you are asked for your assistance in a matter, don't be hesitant about giving it.)

Some of us horde our information and contacts as if they were precious jewels. The more we share with others, the more we ultimately receive ourselves.

Find out someone's special interest, and get that person something related to it as a gift.

It is amazing how little we truly know about those around us, how much time in relationships is spent skimming the surface. Many of us have friends and acquaintances who have all kinds of special, secret interests of which we are unaware.

Today, find out more about the special interests of friends or acquaintances. Do they love model airplanes, gardening, country music, collecting dolls? What kind of books do they like? When you find out what they're particularly interested in, make a special effort to get something for them in that area. It could be something as simple as an article or magazine about their hobby, an old recording, or it could even be a trip with them to a museum that has an exhibit about that interest.

They will feel especially understood by you and touched that you took the time to find out about them and respond in this way.

If someone you know is out of work, try to help them find a job.

Being out of work can be frightening. The person looking for a job never knows how long it will take until a job is found. If you hear that someone has lost their job, take the time and effort to think about who you know who might be able to hire them, or who could lead them to a job possibility. Most jobs are gained by contacts, information, and timing. You might be your friend's best resource.

Make a few phone calls on that friend's behalf. See if you can put the person in touch with others who can help. He or she will be extremely grateful for your efforts at this difficult time, and will know someone is there for them.

Give someone a guest pass to your health club.

So many of us find endless reasons not to start working out. The prospect may seem overwhelming, or we may not have a place to go.

If you belong to a health club (or even if you don't), get a guest pass to a health club for a friend who needs it. Guest passes to health clubs are readily available and will help the person take that important first step. He or she will be shown around, allowed to use the equipment, and may even decide to take an aerobic class. Your friend may feel at home there, enjoy the visit, or even meet a personal trainer who can offer guidance.

Once the first step is made, it is always easier to return. Another benefit is that once you have a friend at the club, you'll probably go there more often yourself.

Help mobilize youth at risk.

A tremendous number of youngsters in our country are living at risk from crime, drug addiction, broken homes, street violence, and general hopelessness. When asked, these youngsters often say they see no future but death or jail by the time they are twenty-one years old.

Reach out and give such a youngster the support he or she needs. Youth at Risk is a nonprofit national and international organization, privately funded, that works with children from fifteen years of age and up who are in trouble with the law, school, and their parents. These children are privately recruited, as are their families and schools. The organization, which operates in thirteen states and also abroad, offers a year of transformational work, where the children and a committed other learn the skills of living and taking responsibility.

Contribute funds or volunteer your time to this or similar organizations that are making the difference between life and death in these youngsters' lives.

Throw a goodbye party for a friend who is moving.

So many people come in and out of our lives in this mobile society. When someone we've been close to moves away, an empty space is left behind. Rather than just let the person go, throw a goodbye party and invite all those people he or she has known.

It is important to commemorate times of change. At the party, you can tell the person who is leaving how much he or she has meant to you. The party always says that departure may be a physical separation, but not the end of a caring friendship.

You will help the person who is leaving to feel supported in undertaking the difficult task of resettling somewhere else.

Visit a nursing home. Bring in the autumn with autumn leaves, pine cones, and other memorabilia.

Many elderly individuals in nursing homes do not have the privilege of going outdoors and appreciating the beauty of autumn. Why not gather autumn together and bring it to them?

Collect autumn leaves, pine cones, fallen tree branches, gourds, corn, and anything else that displays the autumn season, and bring these objects to a nursing home.

Your thoughtfulness, visit, and effort will touch many, making them feel as though they have had a taste of autumn as well.

In honor of De Paali, take a day to be grateful for the money you have received.

De Paali, an important Hindu holiday, celebrates the prosperity received all year long. In preparation, individuals balance their checkbooks and make sure their funds are in order. For the actual celebration, candles are lit all over the house, a feast is prepared, and prayers are offered to Lakshmi, the God of prosperity. Then all celebrate together.

All year long, we receive so much of which we may be unaware. This is a good time to take stock of our funds and give special thanks and acknowledgment for it. It is also a good time to think about how we share our prosperity, and find a new way to give to someone you may not have shared with before.

Pay attention to those running for election. See what the issues are that are being disputed. Choose a candidate that you admire and do one thing to help him or her.

Many of us pay little attention to elections that are held either regionally or nationally. We feel that one vote may not make a difference. However, this is a tremendous mistake.

Each person who puts the time, attention, and energy to finding out who is running and what the issues are at hand is making a vital contribution to the quality of life.

Make a point of finding out who is running for office and what their qualifications are. Become aware of what is being debated. How can you contribute to the dialogue in a meaningful way?

Can you give the candidate time, hand out flyers, arrange to have them meet your friends, make calls to get the vote out? Or perhaps your contribution might be writing letters to the editor of your local newspaper, or creating a petition for others to sign. As more join in more possibilities for solutions can be found.

If you've lost a loved one, allow the grieving to end. Start anew.

A wonderful way to give thanks to life is to be willing to start over again. After the loss of a loved one, it can sometimes be difficult to get out and live again. We need time to grieve and mourn what has been taken from us. However, at some point we must declare that it is time to resume our lives again.

Some hold onto mourning indefinitely. By doing so, they feel as if they are holding onto the person or to memories of a happier time.

Decide today to move on. Allow the loss to be in the past, focus on the new life available now. Be willing to step out, trust, and start once again.

Power resides in the moment of transition from a past to a new state.

—Ralph Waldo Emerson

Buy Girl Scout cookies. Support your local civic organizations when they have drives.

When Girl Scouts come around selling cookies, make sure you buy several boxes. Not only are the cookies delicious, but by participating in civic efforts, you are being a good neighbor and helping the community run well. You can also buy raffles that are offered, and if a civic picnic is scheduled, make sure to attend.

Find a new recipe that you've never made before, and cook it in honor of something special.

To celebrate a special occasion, why not spend time making a brand-new, delicious recipe you've never tried before? Then serve it to your family.

The house will fill with the delicious aroma, and the new meal you are serving will make the occasion particularly festive. All will enjoy and feel nurtured. They will be aware of and appreciate your personal time, thoughtfulness, and effort on everyone's behalf.

Do a puzzle with a child.

Choose some puzzles that are age appropriate for a child you know. Instead of just giving them to the child as a present, sit down on the floor and do some puzzles with the youngster yourself.

In actually working on a project like this with a child, you'll give that child feelings of real support, and you'll be surprised to discover how much the child has to give to you as well.

Give away some old furniture you're not using to someone who needs it.

Most of our homes are cluttered with old pieces of furniture and memorabilia that have not been used for years. It is a wonderful feeling to give up some of these nostalgic items, and even more wonderful to share them with others who could use them. Contact your local Police Athletic League and find out if there is a place in your neighborhood where such furniture is distributed.

You could also just put it out at the front stoop. People who like it or need it will drive by and take it themselves.

OCTOBER 31
Halloween

Make Halloween extra enjoyable for those around you. Make an unusual costume for a child or yourself, scoop out a pumpkin and put it in the window, and get healthy treats for the trick-or-treaters.

Halloween is a time when we can all become anything we'd like to be. Make a costume for a youngster or for yourself that is unusual and fun, someone you or they have always wanted to be like. Some examples could be a unicorn, butterfly, a knight or fair maiden, or a bride.

When children come to the door for tricks or treats, give them only healthy treats. Some examples could be little boxes of raisins, popcorn, dried fruit, corn chips, nuts, and seeds. These are always preferable to candy. Pumpkin seeds in particular make a lovely offering.

Take some time to check in the health food store and learn about all the nourishing goodies that are available, and contribute to a holiday that is healthy as well as fun.

NOVEMBER 1

Stand when someone enters the room or approaches your table.

When someone enters a room to be introduced to you, or comes over to a table where you are seated and you stand up, you are welcoming them in a unique way. Your action gives them honor and respect and, most importantly, acknowledges that their simple presence makes a difference.

In the Bible it says that when you honor those who come into your life you honor the one who sent them. By doing this for another, you are honoring and acknowledging all of life, yourself included. Needless to say, the person being recognized will feel touched and worthwhile too.

Late autumn and winter are a good time for reflection. Buy a beautiful notebook just for you and keep a diary.

Diary writing is cathartic, intimate, and meaningful. Buy yourself a notebook that pleases you and start to keep a diary today. Each day write at least a few words in the diary about issues and thoughts that concern you.

As the days go by you will feel closer to yourself, more aware of what is important, and also that you are becoming a good listener and friend to yourself.

There are books and workshops available on diary keeping. The process can become quite an art and have an extraordinary effect on you.

Start your child (or yourself) on a collection, be it stamps, coins, dolls, rocks, baseball cards, or art.

Collections can be a wonderful way of learning and saving for the future. Getting a child started on a collection can serve that child well for his or her whole life. Not only will the child become knowledgeable in an area, but the collection can easily become more and more valuable over time.

Choose something that is of interest to you or to your child, such as stamps, coins, dolls, rocks, baseball cards, art, or antique furniture. Begin a collection. Be creative about how you do this. Looking for items to add to your collection can involve going on interesting trips, meeting new people, and even studying more history than you would have otherwise.

There will be a sense of fulfillment and gratification for the time and effort wisely spent.

If two people you know are in a fight, do your best to create peace between them.

We like to step aside when people are fighting, feeling it is not our business. However, there may be ways in which we can help to bring the situation to a peaceful conclusion.

Make an effort to intervene and create harmony when two are fighting. Offer new solutions and help them see the situation from a different perspective. Let them know the consequences of keeping their anger going.

Often an outside, calm, objective point of view can make the difference when emotions have reached the boiling point.

Tonight, spend time reviewing your day. Ask yourself, what did I receive today? What did I give today? What trouble did I cause someone? Write the answers down.

These exercises are part of what's called "Naikan introspection." Rather than focus on how we've been wronged, the exercises ask us to reflect on how we might have caused trouble or pain.

As we do these exercises, we realize how much we are receiving all day long, how little we're actually giving. By becoming aware, we become grateful for the many gifts we receive and eager to find ways of giving. Soon it becomes natural to be careful about causing difficulty and harm.

These questions can also be asked about a person or a relationship. Write down your answers and reflect.

When you have faults,
do not fear to abandon them.

—CONFUCIOUS

Go to an orphanage and see if there's a way you can help.

Orphanages and foster homes can usually use all the help and support they can get. The children can be very hungry for the time, attention, and caring they cannot get from their own parents.

Make a point of visiting an orphanage or foster home. Bring some books to read to a child, crafts to do, music, puzzles, or any other activity you would like to share. Offer to go over homework assignments. Spending even a little time with these children can make an enormous difference.

Go to a marathon where others are running or walking, and stand on the sidelines to cheer them on.

It takes months of preparation to run or walk in a marathon. Some participate in marathons to benefit charities, others for personal reasons. Whatever the cause, a great deal is at stake for the runners and walkers, both physically and emotionally.

Participants are empowered by the presence of supporters who stand on the sidelines and cheer them on. Many have said that without the people watching and cheering, they never would have made it.

Be a supporter. Go out and cheer others on.

Willingly help with the household chores without having to be asked.

There are endless chores in a household that need attention regularly, such as doing dishes, sweeping, putting in new lightbulbs, taking out the garbage, making minor repairs, or carrying grocery bags into the house and unpacking them.

It is not fair for the brunt of these tasks to fall on one individual. Help with these chores willingly on a regular basis so that your input can be counted on. Not only does this make things physically easier for others, but the feeling of emotional support generated by doing so will be greatly appreciated.

Become a Pen Pal. Correspond with someone in another part of the nation, another country, or someone who is incarcerated.

There are many Pen Pal organizations and clubs all over the country, such as Pen Pal Planet Free and Pen Pals for USA. These organizations link up individuals who could mutually benefit from corresponding with one another by sharing their thoughts, backgrounds, and struggles on an ongoing basis, and providing mutual support.

Contact an organization in your area, find a pen pal who seems suitable, and develop a new friend. Not only will this expand your horizons, but your own personal experiences can be a source of inspiration and guidance to others too.

If someone is sick, make a special point of visiting them. Bring a basket of goodies along.

A visit from a friend when one is ill can have a really rejuvenating effect. The warmth, caring, and love expressed enters the body and helps the person heal.

When you go on a visit like this, bring a basket of goodies. Find out what the person can have, and bring some for them. A little homemade soup, fresh juice, or baked bread can work wonders.

Go to a Veterans Day parade. Honor those who have sacrificed for their country.

Parades are a way of publicly acknowledging groups of people, actions performed, or special times of importance. Even if you aren't marching yourself, your presence at a parade is important. It adds to the festivities, supports those who are marching, and becomes a way of giving thanks and praise. It also gives you a feeling of belonging and a way of expressing feelings about issues and people who are important to you.

Along with a Veterans Day parade, there are many other parades you can attend, such as the parades for the Fourth of July, Thanksgiving Day, or various national groups who are marching. Pick the ones that are especially meaningful to you, and make a point of going. It will be even more enjoyable if you bring someone else along.

Give everyone breathing room. Give others the chance to have real input into what's going on.

Some of us in the role of authority feel we need to direct and take charge of each person's actions and responses. This leaves little breathing room for others and can make them feel stifled and resentful, like robots. True leadership brings out the best in others. Try to see the task of authority differently.

Today, at work or at home, realize that each person you oversee has wonderful resources of his or her own. Find a way to let that individual have real input and responsibility in decisions that are made. Allow others to find new solutions of their own. As you do this, not only will entire projects thrive, but so will all of you and your relationships.

Learn how to communicate lovingly.

There are many ways to say the same thing. Some of us just blurt out our message in any old way, never giving careful attention to the manner in which we communicate.

When we communicate in a rushed, loud, or angry tone, the person we are speaking to may not ever hear the words we are saying. What is responded to is the manner in which the words are being said.

Take a moment before you communicate to pay attention to the tone, feeling, and manner in which you are delivering your message. Don't put the other person on the defensive. Couch your words in careful phrases. Look the person directly in the eye. Let that person know you care about how he or she responds and that there is time for a reply.

This extra thoughtfulness will pay off. The person will be able to hear you, and also can respond in any way he or she desires.

NOVEMBER 14

If there is something you want from another, ask them directly.

It is very difficult for some of us to ask for what we want directly. We may be terribly afraid of being rejected and having our request refused. Instead of being direct about it, we start to wheel and deal or manipulate, creating confusion and guilt.

This time, simply ask for what you want directly. Be fully prepared to allow time for your request to either be accepted or refused. People have a right to say yes or no, and you have a right to ask.

When you communicate directly, the other person will feel grateful for the opportunity to be treated with respect.

NOVEMBER 15

Don't litter. Make sure you throw gum and candy wrappers, soda cans, newspapers, tissues, paper bags, and other trash in a garbage can.

It is very easy to unconsciously litter and toss our refuse here or there, particularly at beaches, in the car, parks, and along busy city streets. Doing so creates an environment that is messy and unpleasant for those with whom we share it. The overall effect is demoralizing, saying that we neither care about our environment or one another.

It only takes an extra moment or two to make an effort to find a nearby garbage can and put our refuse in it. If everyone took the time to do this, the overall benefit would be tremendous.

NOVEMBER 16

Put other people ahead of yourself.

Most of the time we are thinking about our goals, tasks, achievements, and how we can get ahead. We all want to be special and important. Self-importance can be an impediment to enjoying our lives.

Today, give up having to be important. Instead, put others ahead of you. Think about what others are needing, doing, and feeling instead of what you desire. Some examples could be instead of telling someone of your success, ask about how their projects are going. Give your friend the chance to choose the restaurant, movie, or play to which you are both going.

Being truly aware of and available to others is a beautiful way of really being important.

Give up sirs, your proud airs, your many wishes, and mannerisms and extravagant claims. They won't do you any good, sir. That's all I have to tell you.

—LAO-TZU

NOVEMBER 17

If you have an appointment and can't make it or are running late, call and let the individual know you will be delayed.

Sometimes we simply forget about or don't arrive at a doctor, dentist, barber, or beauty parlor, or any other appointment, and neglect to let the office know. However, their time has been set aside for us. It is time that could have been given to someone else.

If it is impossible to get to an appointment you've made, or you are going to get there late, let the office know as soon as you can. If there is time enough, they may be able to fill the slot. At the very least, the person expecting to see you can plan to use the time in another way.

Everyone's time is precious. Be respectful of it.

If someone comes late to your home or party, don't make that person feel bad about it.

Sometimes a guest will arrive late at a party or dinner invitation or just for a visit. Don't make the person feel bad about it. Welcome your guest whenever he or she comes. Tell the person you understand and that the delay was probably unavoidable. This will ease a tense moment and rescue the entire visit.

If you're throwing a party, make sure everyone there knows each other and is comfortable.

As the host or hostess of a party, it is very important to keep your eye on the guests. Make sure everyone is having a good time and no one is left out. Occasionally a few people can slip through the cracks. They may not know everyone who is present, or may feel alone.

If you notice someone is not joining in, go over to that person. Welcome your guest personally and make sure he or she is introduced to everyone. As you make the introductions, say a few nice things. Let each person know that he or she is appreciated.

Don't lie about small things.

We often feel it is all right to twist the truth a little bit in tiny matters. We think an exaggeration here, a fantasy there, will make things more lively.

However, even small lies build up. They effect others and also ourselves. Lies can obscure action that needs to be taken, or can create confusion in others and yourself. Most people see through lies anyway. Lies make you look foolish.

Be ruthless with yourself about telling lies. Stop whenever you feel it coming. This will help others as well as yourself realize what reality is and do what needs to be done.

Nothing is hidden,
Since ancient times
It is all clear as daylight.
—Zen Saying

Put on a play or puppet show for children in the hospital.

Children who are hospitalized over the holiday season feel particularly deprived and alone. It is rather simple and enjoyable to get a few people together, make silly costumes, and put on a play for a child. You can take this little group into a hospital and perform the play for the children in their lounge.

You could also make or bring puppets and put on a puppet show for the children. All will be delighted. This will bring real festivity to an unhappy time.

THANKSGIVING

Find someone who has no place to go for Thanksgiving and invite them to your holiday meal.

Families are so mobile and disparate these days that many people are left alone on Thanksgiving Day, which is always the fourth Thursday in November. Take some time to ask your neighbors and friends if they have a place to go for Thanksgiving dinner. If they do, make a few phone calls and ask others if they know someone who will be alone. Take the trouble to call up that person and include them at your Thanksgiving table.

A meal prepared only for oneself and family never fills or nourishes as completely as a meal shared with someone in need.

Give your pet extra attention today.

Our pets give us unconditional love no matter how we treat them. Take time today to really honor your pet. Cuddle your cat. Take your dog for an extra long walk. Give your pet a special bath and spend more time playing. You might want to tell your pet how much you love him or her and all he or she means to you. Your pet will get the message and you'll both feel great.

Send some money, objects, or gifts to a Third World country where it is needed.

It is absolutely amazing to realize how far a little bit goes in the Third World. There are millions of men, women, and children who would greatly benefit from whatever small contribution you can make.

UNICEF has many programs through which you could assist, such as the Emergency Relief Fund, which provides nutrition, clothing, and medical attention during times of trouble. The Micro Credit Lending program for developing nations provides loans to buy seed and fertilizer. They harvest their products, sell them for a profit, repay their loans, and use their income to send their children to school and to buy homes.

There are other organizations as well, such as the World Crisis Network and the Red Cross, which could help direct any contribution you care to make.

If something bothers you, talk to the person who can do something about it. Don't tell everyone else.

Some of us tell everyone we know about an event that has troubled us, causing ourselves and others to be generally upset. We seldom go to the person who has caused it, or who is in charge of the situation, and work it out.

It is much more efficient and fruitful not to disturb others, but resolve the problem directly with the person or persons who are involved or in a position to make a change. When you take this new course of action, you will be delighted at how quickly situations get resolved and how much better everyone feels.

Support the environment. Buy holiday cards printed on recycled paper.

We are often unconscious of the many ways in which we devour our natural resources and disregard the environment. We have to remember that paper comes from trees that are cut down. These trees, when allowed to live, naturally cleanse our air. They control the earth's temperature and water levels as well.

Buy holiday cards this year that are printed on recycled paper. Each time you do so you avoid making a demand for fresh paper that comes from killing another tree.

Prepare a gift for everyone who will be at your holiday meal.

We normally do not exchange gifts at Thanksgiving, but why not start a new custom? What a nice way of saying thank you.

Gifts can be simple: something small that catches your eye, little pottery bowls, dried flowers. Wrap the surprises nicely and tie them with a colorful bow.

What a lovely addition they will make to the festivities.

Get to know someone from a different culture. Invite them to your home.

It is fascinating to open our doors to people of other nations and cultures. Make a point of inviting someone from a different culture to your home for a meal and really get to know them. If you don't immediately know someone from another culture, contact a club, school, or association. Call the Chamber of Commerce in your community and ask for the names and phone numbers of organizations that serve African Americans; Japanese, Chinese, or Korean Americans; Native Americans, or any other cultural or racial group that is of interest to you. Attend a few meetings. Make brand-new friends.

This will make the person feel so much more a part of this country, and it will also open your horizons to experiences you could not have in any other way.

There must be no tolerance of intolerance.
—KARL JASPERS

If two people are having difficulties with each other, do all you can to help them work it out.

Most of us do not want to get involved in the personal difficulties of others, fearing our participation will backfire one way or another. However, if two people are telling you about their difficulties, rather than walk away from them, do all you can to help them work it out.

A sympathetic listener is worth a great deal, especially if you don't take sides. Sometimes, just the chance to have a third party listen can alter the balance by itself. At other times, gentle advice from a respected friend can go a long way to seeing possibilities that might have been overlooked.

When you are willing to actively involve yourself in another's pain, the benefit extends back to you, causing you to become wiser, stronger, and more compassionate.

Give work to others during the holiday season.

There are many extra expenses people have during the holiday season. If you can, offer work for pay during this time so others have a chance to earn extra funds.

Some work you might need could include baby-sitting, home repairs, landscaping, house painting, cooking, tailoring, and so on. Put a notice in your local paper. The extra income will be greatly appreciated by many at this time of year.

Mend little rips and tears in your relationships.

Is there someone you haven't called back for a while? Or someone else with whom you never made that luncheon date, although you promised to do so? Have you been putting off a visit? Unfinished business in our relationships can become little rips and tears, making the fabric of the relationship less sturdy with time.

Put time aside to make overdue calls. Schedule that visit. Arrange for that luncheon appointment. Not only will you feel much better about yourself, but you'll enjoy the renewed and improved contact with those you care about as well.

Have faith in others. Tell others a story of a time when faith triumphed in your life.

The Jewish holiday of Hanukkah, which falls in the month of December, is about miracles and faith. A small group defeated a huge army arrayed against them with the power of faith. A candle, which was supposed to burn one night, lasted eight nights, giving comfort, hope, and warmth.

Each night an additional candle is lit as the miracle is remembered. These candles are to be made public, as are stories of triumph through faith. Our lives must also be like those candles, burning strongly through times of doubt and fear.

Tell others a story in your life when everything was against you and yet you triumphed through faith. Develop faith in others as well, to defeat the great enemy of cynicism.

See what gifts you can make instead of buy. Give extra thought to each gift you plan to give for the holidays. Make each one unique and personal.

Many of us rush out to buy whatever we can for the people on our gift list, thinking that the more elaborate or expensive the gift, the better it is. This can be a way to avoid giving a real gift.

This year, spend time to really personalize your gifts. It is not the cost but the thought and care involved that makes a gift special.

See how many gifts you can make instead of buy. Perhaps you could even take the money you saved in this manner and donate it to a worthy cause.

Learn how to make a gingerbread house and give it away as a present.

Feed any birds that may still be around.

Gingerbread houses are wonderful for the holidays. They are usually made of gingerbread and decorated with candy canes, marshmallows, candy, raisins, and all kinds of other assorted treats.

It is not very difficult to make one of your own. Look at different gingerbread houses. Get a book about them which includes recipes. Pick a type you like and see if you can make a few. (In some cities, there are classes and workshops available on decorating gingerbread houses. Look in newspapers and magazines to see if there are any workshops listed in your city.)

Gingerbread houses really spice up the holidays and make fabulous gifts.

There are many small birds in winter who would benefit greatly from bird seed or bread crumbs you might leave around.

Put a bird feeder in your backyard or apartment window. Fill it regularly, and have the double pleasure of enjoying the visits of these birds and knowing you are helping with their hunger.

Pay special attention to your mother-in-law and father-in-law. Let them know you are grateful for the job they did raising your spouse.

There is often competition and conflict between mothers-in-law and fathers-in-law. Sometimes these relationships can interfere with a marriage.

In preparation for the holiday season of thanks and good will, make a special effort to reach out to your in-laws. Tell them how much you appreciate all the years they spent raising your spouse. Acknowledge and honor them in other ways too. Find qualities they have that you respect, like what fine grandparents they are, or how thoughtful they have been to your mate, and make a point of mentioning it to them.

Appreciation and acknowledgment go a long way in defusing conflict and strain. The in-laws will feel appreciated and closer to you, as if you are all on the same team. Rifts that may have been forming will be mended.

Promote good will and understanding among people of different religions. Invite someone of a different faith to your holiday celebration.

During this holiday season, when so many different religious holidays are being celebrated, it is in the spirit of all the religions to see how you can promote good will and understanding, rather than have differences be a source of separation and fear.

Invite those of a different religion to your home and share your holiday with them. Explain what it's about. Go to the home and communities of those of different religions and learn what is meaningful to them. Some communities have Interfaith Centers, where all can get together to share and understand different paths more deeply.

Whatever promotes love and understanding is in the best interest of all.

DECEMBER 6

Think of someone who hasn't been able to forgive you. Write down the reasons why and see if you have corrected them. Forgive yourself.

When someone is consistently angry with us and hasn't been able to forgive us, it can affect us in many ways. On some level we feel it. The unresolved anger can affect other areas of our lives.

Think of someone who hasn't been able to forgive you. Write down the reasons why from their point of view. If there is any validity in their reasons, see if you have corrected them. If not, correct them now. Do this until you are no longer guilty in your own eyes.

Then contact the person and explain what you've done. Perhaps they will be ready to forgive you now. If not, once you've made the corrections you will be able to forgive yourself and move on.

DECEMBER 7

Be aware of all those who have touched you this year. Make a list of what they have done. On your holiday greeting card, make a point of writing a special note acknowledging each person's contribution to your life.

Rather than just sending a routine holiday card, take the time to write a special note on the card to those who have particularly touched you this year. Acknowledge who they are and the specific contribution they made.

This kind of message is itself a gift. It can mean much more than any material thing they receive.

A friend is a present you give yourself.
—ROBERT LOUIS STEVENSON

DECEMBER 8

See others as they can be, not as they are now.

The way we perceive other people often dictates the way they react both to us and to themselves. We can draw positive or negative aspects out of anyone. People who dwell upon the flaws in others are creating self fulfilling prophecies.

Today, see others as they can be. See them as strong, beautiful, healthy, and good. The more you dwell on those parts of their nature, the more than will express those qualities to you. Your positive perception of them will also help them feel valued and actualize their best traits.

DECEMBER 9

Plan a holiday party that is entirely different this year. Invite new people. Do different things.

Rather than just repeat old habits, it is enlivening to find new ways of celebrating holidays. This causes us to think more about the meaning of the holidays.

When planning your holiday festivities this year, do some things that are new. Include people that you haven't invited before. Have an open house if you don't usually do that, or perhaps a holiday brunch. Take your whole family on a short trip out of town to visit relatives you haven't seen for a while.

It's good to vary our ways of celebrating. This allows us to include more people and shows aspects of the holiday we may not have seen before.

This year find or make unusual gift wrappings.

The way a gift is wrapped says as much as the gift itself. It shows time, thoughtfulness, and personal attention. By doing so, you express how much the person means to you.

It is fun to find or make special gift wrappings. You can use colored tissue papers, rice paper, newspapers covered with sprinkles, all kinds of ribbons and bows. There is no end to what is possible.

Once the gift is wrapped, tie ornaments on it, such as lollipops, candy canes, or balloons.

When the person receives the gift, the wrapping makes it even more important. Your feeling speaks for itself.

Many people have a hard time during the holiday season. Have a few extra preholiday dinners and be mindful to invite those who seem unhappy.

Take the time to be aware of those you know who may feel they are alone or having a difficult time. If they cannot join you during your main dinner or celebration, have a few extra preholiday dinners or gatherings and invite them. Perhaps they would enjoy helping you decorate your home for the holidays. They could bring their own decorations or cook a few dishes as well. This will make the person feel needed, wanted, and more a part of what is going on.

Offer to spend time taking care of young children so that their parents have more time to prepare for their holiday.

The care of young children can be so demanding that it becomes difficult for parents to get away for even a short time to prepare for their holiday season. If you know a couple with young children, why not offer to care for the children so they can count on some free time to spend on their holiday preparations.

This is really a wonderful gift and will be greatly appreciated.

Donate old winter clothing and canned goods to the Salvation Army.

Get a bag and fill it with old winter clothing and canned goods. You can also ask friends, family and coworkers to contribute something to it. Many times, others are happy to contribute if someone else takes the initiative.

When the gift bag is filled to the brim, bring it to the Salvation Army or to any other organization or group that you would like to acknowledge in a special way.

Make a point of meeting and really getting to know someone whose group you have been prejudiced against.

Prejudice is a toxic emotion based on blindness; it has a way of spreading into many parts our lives. It's unfair to both ourselves and others, and it limits the range of our experience.

Make a point of undoing prejudice. Meet and really get to know someone in a group against whom you have been prejudiced. Spend some time with this person. Find out about his or her struggles and dreams. Look at the ways in which the two of you are similar.

In every group, there are both wonderful and difficult individuals. It's crucial to realize that generalization about an entire group is misguided and leads to many wrongs.

Include the memory of those who have passed away in your holiday season. Put pictures of them around and talk about their lives and the lessons they imparted. Honor them.

The holiday season is a wonderful time to include memories of those who have died and to acknowledge once again the gifts and lessons they brought into our lives. Doing this will diminish the sense of loss we have and bring a feeling of continuity. By remembering and speaking of those who have departed, we keep them with us, sharing our life journey.

Designate a certain amount of time each day for reflection, prayer, or meditation. During this busy season, time for stillness is crucial for all.

The holiday season can become frantic with rounds of parties, shopping, card sending, and phone calls. It is most crucial during a time like this to carefully designate special time for reflection, quiet, rest, prayer, or meditation. Time spent in this manner will enhance the quality of the celebrations and insure that you do not become overwhelmed.

Don't give up on a person.

It is easy to get discouraged or overwhelmed by a difficult person or situation. Many reach their breaking point and then just give up.

Don't give up on a person. It often looks the darkest just before a time of change. Stay with a difficult person or situation. Keep on giving as much as you can. Provide words of encouragement. Try not to judge. Nothing stays the same forever. There is always a solution if we persevere long enough.

Do good at all times
For you can never call back a day
To perform a good deed that was neglected.

—Jain Scriptures

DECEMBER 18

Go sledding and take others along.

It's wonderful to be a part of the snowy winter season by sledding with those we love. Everyone bundles up warmly and enjoys the snow, the hills, and the ride together.

This keeps in mind the many simple, inexpensive pleasures that life provides for us.

DECEMBER 19

After a snowstorm, while cleaning the ice and snow off your car, clean off another car nearby. If you have to shovel out your car, do the same for a neighbor.

Once we are cleaning the ice and snow off our own car, it doesn't take much extra effort to reach out and clean off a nearby car as well. Usually, it takes only a few more minutes to shovel out another car.

The person we helped in this manner will be extremely grateful. Think how delighted you would be at this kind of surprise.

Fast, or eat more sparingly for part of the day, in honor of Ramadan. Tell others about it.

Trust that you are protected. Tell it to others.

The Islamic holiday Ramadan, which lasts an entire month and can fall at any time of year, comprises a month of fasting. No food is taken during daylight hours. During this month, there is also fasting from sex, lust, hypocrisy, backbiting, and lies. It is a time of purification of body and spirit, a time to fast from anything that distracts from the remembrance of God.

To appreciate this tradition, eat sparingly yourself for a day or two. Experience both the physical and spiritual effects of fasting. Tell others about it and, if you can, fast with a friend.

It is simple to go through life feeling unprotected and vulnerable to the many negative things we hear all day long. Living this way only generates suspicion and fear.

Trust that you are protected. Trust that there is a higher force that guides our steps and our days. Do not focus upon or expect trouble to come. Expect the best. When others say otherwise, tell them that they are protected too.

Look closely at what did and didn't work for you this past year and decide on a truly new direction in one area of your life.

The end of the year is a natural time for reviewing our activities, projects, and efforts during the past year.

Look closely at what did and didn't work for you. What were the fruits of your deeds? Were your resources used to their fullest extent? Were you all that you could be?

Find an area that was not to your liking and decide on a truly new direction in the coming year. Sketch the new direction out on paper. What steps will this new direction require? An example might be dealing with food, weight, or exercise. We might study more about nutrition, and join a gym or health club where we may look into working with a personal trainer or nutritionist.

As we give thought to the direction our lives are taking, we realize we are always the captain of our ships. If we are in murky waters, we can change course at any time.

Buy a blank book, fill it with inspiring quotes, and give it as a gift to someone.

Take some time to collect sayings and quotations that have inspired you. Bringing them all together in one place will have additional impact, both for you and others.

Unless quotes are read and absorbed regularly, they tend to be forgotten, easily drifting out of consciousness. The process of finding those that are meaningful to you and gathering them together will implant them more strongly in your mind. The more vivid they are to you, the more they will impact your actions.

Once your collection of quotes is complete, buy another blank book and make a copy of it. Give the copy to a friend as a gift.

DECEMBER 23

Bring holiday gifts to those in the hospital or in nursing homes.

It is hard to spend holidays in the hospital or alone in nursing homes. Some patients have few visitors. Others know they face difficulties in the coming year.

Gather some gifts and packages together and go to your local hospital or nursing home and find out what the procedure is for distributing them.

Even a few hours spent in this manner will be rewarding for all concerned.

DECEMBER 24
Christmas Eve

Read from the Bible, parables, or some book of spiritual significance for you.

Christmas Eve is a time of togetherness with friends and families. Sometimes there is a family dinner; other times there are parties with friends.

This is a perfect occasion to read from the Bible, parables, or some book of spiritual significance for you to remind us that we are spiritual beings. If it is appropriate, you might read out loud and share these thoughts with others. This will give extra depth to the celebration and open the possibility of discussion about the meaning of Christmas in everyone's life.

DECEMBER 25
Christmas

Have an open house party for all to attend.

This is a time for sharing, giving, and making friends. An open house is a lovely way of reconnecting with friends you haven't seen for awhile and of nurturing relationships with new people you've met recently. Some people like to tell those they invite to feel free to bring along family and friends. When you do this, your circle of friendship widens. There's no telling what wonderful person will walk in the door. A new friend is the best present of all.

DECEMBER 26
Kwanza

Learn about the celebration of Kwanza, the African-American holiday. Find ways it could relate to your life and tell others about it.

Kwanza is a seven-day festival developed by Maulana Karenga in 1966. Based on the traditional African harvest festival, it emphasizes the role of family and community in African-American culture. Each day is dedicated to a particular principle: unity, self-determination, collective work, responsibility, cooperative economics, purpose, and creativity.

On each day one of the candles in a seven-branched candelabrum is lit. The holiday also includes the giving of gifts and a Karamo African feast.

If you care to, participate in this celebration by dedicating your days to one or another of these principles. For example, for the principle of purpose, spend the day considering the overall purpose of your activities. For the day dedicated to creativity, find one way of enhancing your creative expression during the coming year.

Send photos of yourself and family to relatives and acquaintances who live far away.

Reunite two people who haven't seen each other for a long time.

Photos of yourself and family are a wonderful way to keep in touch with those who have moved far from you or those who you haven't seen in a while. For a short time, you bring yourself back into their life.

Get some pictures that you are proud of, make copies, and send them to friends and relatives you haven't seen recently who would enjoy the pleasure of seeing how you and your family have grown.

If you know two people who haven't seen one another for a long time, this is the perfect season to reunite them. You could tell them in advance, or make it a surprise. Perhaps you might like to invite both of them over quietly, and then let the evening or afternoon take its own course.

DECEMBER 29

Be the first one to say hello, smile, and invite someone to lunch.

Often we wait for another to give us a smile, say hello, or extend an invitation of some kind. When these gestures do not come, we are left feeling alone. What we do not realize is that the other person is probably also waiting for us to make a similar move.

Today, give to another what you want for yourself. Be the first one to smile, say hello, or extend an invitation to lunch. The other person will most probably be delighted and respond in kind. And you will have broken the ice.

One word frees us
From all the weight and pain of life;
That word is love.

—SOPHOCLES

DECEMBER 30

Call up three old friends you haven't seen for a while and wish them a happy new year. Make plans to see each other again soon.

It is easy to lose track of old friends. People move away, misunderstandings escalate, and new friends or interests can absorb our attention.

Call up three old friends you haven't seen for a while. Wish them a happy new year. Find out what's going on in their lives. Tell them you wish them well. If at all possible, make plans to see each other soon.

189

DECEMBER 31
New Year's Eve

Don't drink on New Year's Eve if you're driving home. Drink eggnog, apple cider, or hot chocolate. Protect yourself and others.

Drinking and driving often mean death on the road. What an awful way to end the year. Be vigilant and mindful about this. There are many nonalcoholic drinks that are delicious to enjoy at a New Year's Eve celebration. Have eggnog, apple cider, hot chocolate, or whatever. If you are the designated driver, don't go near alcohol. Protect yourself and others on the road so that all can live to have a happy, healthy New Year.